WHAT HAPPENED TO YOU?

A SOLO WHEELCHAIR TRAVEL MEMOIR

SYLVIA LONGMIRE

PRINTED IN THE UNITED STATES OF AMERICA

Find out what happened to me at www.spintheglobe.net.

First edition published in 2021.

Book design by Sylvia Longmire.

Editing by Kelsey Tressler.

Cover Image: ©Sylvia Longmire

ISBN: 978-1-7345113-2-1

DEDICATION

To Jackson and PJ, the most amazing travel companions any wheelchair mom could possibly hope for.

CONTENTS

PREFACE

One of the greatest ironies of writing a travel memoir in the middle of a pandemic is realizing you haven't traveled anywhere in over a year. It also doesn't help matters when you don't know what travel will look like the next time you try it. Yet, here I am, tapping away at my laptop keyboard while ensconced in self-isolation since early March 2020. It's absolutely insane that I'm actually excited about the prospect of getting on a plane again, and don't even get me started on the excruciating pain in my gut caused by cruise withdrawal. But, oddly enough in this extraordinary circumstance, I'm comforted by reliving some of the best and most memorable moments of my life as I put them down on paper. That being said, the journey of writing this book commenced well before the lockdowns.

I started traveling as a wheelchair user in 2015, and began writing the first stories in this book in 2018. Each year, I found myself traveling more frequently, longer distances, and for more extended periods. I had been investing and saving money for two decades, and seeing as I'm technically retired with a military disability pension, it was time to start using that money—especially since I didn't know how much longer my body would physically allow me to travel. So, between February 2016 and March 2020, I visited forty-eight countries (thirty-four by myself), 176 cities, flew 444,714 miles, and spent 522 days away from home. It's best if I don't tell you how much I had to dig into my retirement savings to do this.

Since no one could have predicted the COVID-19 pandemic, I'm glad I trusted my gut and did as much traveling as my body—and my wallet—could possibly handle. After I knocked every international destination off of my bucket list, I started visiting places just because they had a smidgen of wheelchair accessibility. New accessible tour company? Sign me up! Brand-new cruise ship launching? Let's go check it out! These are the decisions you make when you know your ability to travel is irreversibly limited.

During these years I've spent traveling as a wheelchair user, I've been to some incredible destinations and seen some extraordinary things. I've been to the Top of the World on the Burj Khalifa's observation deck in Dubai and I've watched a performance on the steps of the Sydney Opera House down under. I've been on a jet ferry navigating through the fjords of Norway and landed on glaciers in Alaska and Iceland in a helicopter. I've observed the glittering magic of midnight skylines in Singapore and Shanghai and road-tripped through some of the most breathtaking canyon country in the western United States.

But while the sights and sounds I've experienced are the things of travelers' dreams, they're not what made my travel experiences unique. Any two or ten or hundred people can take identical photos of the Eiffel Tower, or the Empire State Building, or the Egyptian pyramids. What makes someone's travel experience one-of-a-kind is the people they meet along the way. You'll soon discover that those people are the real gems in this book.

That's not to say that my wheelchair—and everything that goes along with traveling in it—only has a walk-on role (pun intended). This is, after all, a solo wheelchair travel memoir. It draws heavily from my experience writing about the accessibility of my destinations for my travel blog over the last five years. However, traveling solo in a wheelchair isn't just about finding ramps and getting pissed off at stairs. Every potential interaction with strangers is either magic or disaster waiting to happen (and fortunately, much more of the former than the latter). In foreign countries, I never know how people will perceive me, especially since in some places, a woman traveling alone on wheels is as common as an alien encounter. Then, there are the "fun" moments when people I've never met feel the need to ask me (with no introduction whatsoever), "What happened to you?"

The pages you're about to read are filled with stories about these encounters. Some are funny (at least, *I* think so), some are thought-provoking, and some are downright gut-wrenching. Sometimes my wheelchair and disability are central to the story and sometimes they're only tangential. But the one constant is people, and more specifically, the essential things I've learned about the world (and myself) from them.

So, sit back, relax, and enjoy your flight across my travel memories as I tell you exactly what happened to me.

1 THE ROAD TO LETTING GO

When you get married, you never think about getting divorced. Until you do.

I got married in October 2004, three months before getting diagnosed with MS. I was married for ten years, and like every relationship, it had its ups and downs. Unfortunately, the downs greatly outnumbered the ups toward the end, and our marriage became unsustainable. Looking back, I honestly believe that getting divorced is one of the most difficult and painful things many people have to endure. But, despite all of the emotional hardship that comes along with divorce, I'm eternally grateful for the relationship that produced my greatest treasures—my two incredible sons.

Even though I knew I was doing the right thing by choosing divorce, it was one of the scariest times of my life. My heart was shattering into a million pieces over thoughts of how this would affect our two children, who were six and four at the time. Their father is in the military, and while we were living in Arizona back then, our divorce would coincide with his move to Alabama. I would most likely move to Florida to be near my family, which raised many questions about physical custody.

Sadly, the subject of people with disabilities having, adopting, or parenting children is still taboo. Many people think we are automatically incapable of being good parents because we may lack certain physical abilities. This perception is so pervasive that it's deeply entrenched in both family and divorce court proceedings. In many states, including Arizona, where I was getting divorced, judges can consider a parent's disability when making custody decisions. Family courts can also take children away from disabled parents based on completely subjective criteria determining their fitness.

Like many people in American society, I always assumed I would get primary physical custody of my children because, well…I'm the mom. Also, with their dad in the military, he would be subject to deployments and unusual hours, making it logistically difficult for him to be a full-time single dad. I started scrutinizing my finances, trying to figure out how I would make things work on my own, especially knowing I would have to hire someone to help me take care of them. I knew that, at least in Florida, I would be surrounded by several family members who could provide us with a lot of support. But I still had this sinking feeling in my gut that my boys would potentially be missing out on so many things without a fully able-bodied mother. The combination of my ex-husband's strong desire for primary physical custody and my knowledge that the family court system was stacked against me led to the most painful decision of my life. I let my children go.

In the summer of 2015 while I waited for the divorce to be finalized, I drove across the country and moved to Florida to be near my family. At the same time, my ex-husband and our kids were moving to Alabama for his next Air Force assignment. This meant I would no longer be able to see my children every day— after seven years of not spending more than a handful of days away from them; of taking them to school every day; taking them to Boy Scouts and soccer games; reading to them every night. I was losing all of this simply because I was in a wheelchair. I still can't write about this time in my life without crying.

One could understand that the last thing on my mind after my divorce and subsequent move across the country to Florida was travel. All I wanted to do was cocoon myself in my new home and surround myself with family. For the first time in eighteen years, I didn't have to worry about moving somewhere else in two years. I was back in my home state, and even though

I wasn't familiar with the Orlando area, it was comforting to be surrounded once more by the Earth's greens and blues after the desert southwest's drab browns and grays. I wanted to settle in, I wanted to heal, and I wanted to make a new life for myself. After spending five days in a car driving more than two thousand miles, I didn't want to go anywhere for a long time. Until I did.

Travel means different things to different people, and often changes across the stages of life. The same person could spend her college years backpacking across Europe on twenty dollars a day, partying in Las Vegas with her friends in her twenties, visiting theme parks with her family in her thirties and forties, and going on Mediterranean cruises in her sixties. Some people travel for education, escape, relaxation, adventure, healing, hedonism, holidays, business, or family. Before I became disabled, I traveled at some point for every reason listed above. As a disabled traveler who now uses a wheelchair full-time, I travel simply because I still can. But after my divorce, I didn't know if I could.

Given that I lived an 8-hour drive from my boys after our post-divorce moves, I found myself with a lot of alone time between visits. After spending almost every day of my life for the past several years with my children, the absence was excruciating. Even worse, it was accompanied by no small amount of guilt— guilt for not being there every day, guilt for potentially leading them to believe I abandoned them, and guilt for not being able to make it work with their father. This alone time led me to start contemplating my first post-divorce leisure trip in October 2015. I needed to go somewhere I could be by myself for long stretches; somewhere I could let go of some things and heal.

I needed to go back to the desert.

In 2000, I went to Arizona for the first time, and I went solo. I saw the Grand Canyon, the Painted Desert, and even went on a river float trip where we put in at the base of the Glen Canyon Dam, right on the Arizona-Utah state line. I had never been to that part of the country before, and I felt something while I was there. I grew up Catholic, so I'm not supposed to believe in past lives. Still, I felt some kind of connection to the land and the Native American spirituality around me—specifically the Navajo people. I knew little about their history and had never been exposed to information about their culture, but I did know that something intangible was pulling at me in that desert.

When I started planning my post-divorce trip, I thought back to that pull I'd felt in Arizona many years earlier. It seemed like the perfect place to help me heal, so I chose Monument Valley as the centerpiece of my next excursion. It would be a road trip in early November starting in Phoenix, heading north for a stop in Sedona, then east to Monument Valley for two days. Next, a quick stop at the Four Corners monument, north to Moab to see the Canyonlands and Arches National Parks, west through the San Rafael Swell, then north to fly out of Salt Lake City. At the time, I could still take a few steps with the help of a walker or cane while leaning on my car. It was difficult and not particularly safe, but I could still disassemble my scooter, put the pieces in the trunk of my car, and then shuffle to the driver's seat and use hand controls to drive. Due to fatigue, I would have a limited number of opportunities to take my scooter out of my rental car each day to explore, so I'd have to make them count.

Before I could move on to the wide-open spaces of the Arizona desert after arriving in Phoenix, I needed to make a stop in Sedona. This small but quickly expanding town off Highway 89A is a mecca for spiritualists, psychics, energy practitioners, and healers worldwide. Sedona is home to four major energy vortexes (called as such there, and not the proper *vortices*) that are said to exude funnels of positivity from deep within the Earth. People travel from all over to this quirky desert town—and in rapidly increasing numbers from the growth I saw since my first visit in 2000—to interact with and benefit from these powerful energy flows. I'm primarily drawn to Sedona for its famous red rock landscape that stands in beautiful contrast to the unexpectedly lush surrounding greenery. However, this was a journey of release and healing, so I made an appointment to see a Native American energy practitioner.

Linda was probably in her fifties with long gray hair, no makeup, and a very soothing demeanor. She had Mexican and Apache heritage, and had been a practicing healer for over twenty years. I didn't know what to expect or what to do, so once I got settled in the dark spa therapy room, we just started talking. About thirty minutes into our session, I started emotionally letting go of things I didn't know I had been holding back—mostly pain, guilt, and fear. Pain from my failed marriage and recently broken heart, guilt from not being with my children every day, and a debilitating fear of the future. I exploded with tears and sobs I had no idea I had been holding back.

After we finished talking, Linda started an Apache ritual that I can't even begin to describe with proper accuracy. It involved burning sage, Apache chants, and eagle feathers. But the most critical part of the session was the creation of a small offering—a little earth-friendly cloth-wrapped packet that contained symbols of all the things I was letting go, as well as symbols of my hopes and dreams for the future. I was to place this packet somewhere as an offering to the Native American spirits, and I would know where and when the right time would be to do this. I left that room—and Sedona—light as a feather with an open heart and a renewed sense of purpose.

My words could never do justice to the beauty and awe-inducing grandeur of the landscapes I witnessed in the ensuing days. I woke myself up two mornings in a row at 6 AM so I could watch the sunrise behind the solitary and majestic snow-dusted buttes of Monument Valley. I planted my feet (and electric scooter wheels) in four states at once at the Four Corners monument. I followed the snaking curves of the Colorado River at the bottom of the majestic canyons of Dead Horse Point State Park. I drove two hours without seeing another human being while driving through Canyonlands National Park.

Monument Valley, however, was the absolute highlight. I was to spend the day with a Navajo guide, as that's the only way you can tour the area. It was a chilly but crystal clear day without a cloud in the sky. There was a very light dusting of snow on the ground from the night before, and because it was the off-season, you could hear a pin drop in many spots. We started by driving around the towering spires and buttes, which have famously been featured in dozens of films, from *Stagecoach* and *Easy Rider* to *Forrest Gump* and *Mission: Impossible 2*. It was truly amazing to contemplate how all of these rock formations were created by running water over so many millions of years.

At the beginning of our day together, I told my Navajo guide the story of the offering I had created a few days earlier, and that I had a feeling his tribe's park was where it was meant to be placed. He understood, and agreed to help me. During the second half of our day, we drove slowly next to a natural arch that was still sprinkled with snow at its base. But something was different about this arch, as well as the butte next to it. Looking back, I think it was the rare and solitary juniper tree at the base of the butte. To me, it was a symbol of life; of struggling against the brutal elements above and around to sprout, grow, and prosper. Yes; this was the spot.

I asked my guide to stop the truck, and if it would be okay to bury my offering here. He agreed, took my offering, and got out of the truck. He approached the tree, knelt down, and dug a small hole with his hands right next to the juniper's roots. He placed my packet in the ground, covered it up, and returned to the truck with a gentle smile on his face. He asked me how I felt, and I replied with one word: *Peaceful.*

The rest of my solo road trip was incredible. I started growing more comfortable with the silence and the solitude. I sat in my scooter among these towering rock giants and looked over the edge into endless canyons, feeling incredibly small. My pain and guilt and fear, which had weighed so heavily and loomed so large in my life, seemed insignificant in a place that had stood and evolved over millennia. I wasn't even a blink in time in a place like this, but it was *my* blink, and I finally felt like I had control over what I could do with it. So, I chose to let go.

Today, my sons are thirteen and ten years old. They're intelligent, funny, athletic, kind, and compassionate. Their father got remarried, and they now have a wonderful "bonus mom" and stepbrother who love them. My boys and I are incredibly close despite our physical distance, and they've become astute travel companions who enthusiastically welcomed the bite of their mom's travel bug. But most importantly, they're happy.

I don't know if I'll ever go back to Monument Valley, let alone that juniper tree where hopefully my offering still sits. But I do believe the spirits have been watching over me ever since.

2 YOU REMIND ME OF MY DAUGHTER

For someone terrified of flying and her wheelchair being destroyed by an airline, planning a trip involving a 16-hour plane ride might not seem like a great idea.

Yet, this was what I chose to do for my first international trip as a wheelchair user. Call it a go-big-or-go-home moment that sounded *great* on paper. It wasn't some lifelong dream to visit the Middle East; ironically, I managed to avoid an Air Force deployment to Iraq in 2004 because I was on the verge of getting diagnosed with multiple sclerosis. But my travel goals have always centered on the destination because, let's face it—the people who buy into the cliché that travel is more about the journey are *clearly* not wheelchair users.

In December 2015, I had been living on my own as a full-time "wheelie" for only a few months. A month earlier, I had taken a solo road trip through Arizona and Utah that lasted a week, and while there were some physically challenging moments, it reminded me why I loved traveling so much. I also discovered how much I enjoyed writing about my strange life with MS, and began documenting my days in the deserts and canyons on a little blog that no one knew (or cared) about. I came home from Arizona and went back to focusing on getting my new life as a divorcée and part-time single mom into a routine. Then, I made a huge mistake. I checked Facebook.

My good friends Tom and Rebecca work in education;

Tom is a high school teacher, and Rebecca is a college professor. They got a contract to teach for two years in Dubai, United Arab Emirates, starting in August 2015, and as an active social media user, I was drooling over all the fantastic photos they were posting. I mean, I had friends living in Dubai! They were going on desert safaris, dining and drinking at luxurious Friday brunches, and just doing cool-sexy-amazing things in general. Isn't this what celebrities do on reality TV shows? I was happy that they were having such a good time, but jealous that it wasn't *me* in those photos.

As soon as I found out where they were going to be living, I started half-joking that I was going to visit them. Free room, right? Plus, they were (more or less) inviting all their friends and family to stay with them. I was a friend! Then in September 2015, Emirates Airlines began flying direct from Orlando (my hometown) to Dubai. That was when, as the cool kids say, shit got real for this recovering world traveler. If I did this, it would be my first international trip in six years and my first time traveling to a foreign country with MS—and as a wheelchair user.

If you're not familiar with Dubai at all, you might think visiting any Middle Eastern city is a pipe dream for a person in a wheelchair. I can assure you it is not. Nothing much in Dubai has been around for more than thirty years. In the 1980s, what is now Dubai was a sparsely populated desert. Now, it looks like Disney World and Las Vegas had a love child, and Beverly Hills hosted the baby shower. Since everything is more or less brand new, most hotels, restaurants, tourist attractions, and public sites are wheelchair accessible—except for the sidewalks, but that's another story.

I booked my 16-hour nonstop Orlando-to-Dubai flight for late February 2016, and the second I got the email confirmation, the terror and dread set in. *WHAT THE FUCK DID I JUST DO?!?* The longest flight I had ever been on was ten hours from Rome to JFK airport in New York City, and that was in 2002 when I was fit and healthy. *Would I be able to get a bulkhead seat to accommodate my leg spasms? How would I get to the bathroom? Would I get any sleep?* These are only a few of the dozens of questions we wheelies ask ourselves before we travel. I had three months to go before my flight, and already my stomach was tying itself in knots.

Flying is generally an unpleasant experience for the best of us, but for wheelchair users, it can be our worst nightmare. Our biggest concern is that our wheelchairs will get damaged or lost in the process. If you can believe this, US airlines break or lose approximately twenty-five wheelchairs *every single day*. That's the equivalent of twenty-five passengers having their legs broken by baggage handlers upon arriving at their destination. If I arrive somewhere and my wheelchair is broken, I'm left stranded and helpless, losing all my freedom and independence. I'm also forced to turn around and go home, my travel dreams in pieces next to my chair.

Many people can theoretically understand why a broken wheelchair would put a dent in our travel plans. However, very few non-disabled people understand the personal hell many of us have to go through during the flight. For example, many wheelchair users physically can't use the bathroom, more formally known as a lavatory, on an airplane. Some of us can because we can physically transfer to a tiny (and often rickety) folding on-board wheelchair, also known as *(*cough* a torture device *cough*)* an aisle chair. Flight attendants can't help us in the bathroom, so we have to either transfer to the toilet and clean up by ourselves, or have a travel companion who can assist us.

And if using the lavatory is not an option for you? Then you can use a catheter, pee in a bottle under a blanket (I would only recommend doing this if you're biologically male), or starve and dehydrate yourself for at least twelve hours prior to your flight. Otherwise, you're limited to very short domestic flights, and longer international flights would be virtually impossible.

On my seemingly endless flight, I was, fortunately, able to use the airplane bathroom via aisle chair twice without incident. I got *maybe* a grand total of two hours of sleep, which isn't surprising since I rarely sleep on any flight. And no, I wasn't able to get a bulkhead seat to accommodate my frequent MS-induced leg spasms, so I was squeezed into a regular coach seat for sixteen hours—thankfully with no one sitting next to me. That still didn't help with the legroom situation, and sadly I didn't discover the miracle of premium economy about a year later.

However, I forgot all about the discomfort of my flight once we started our descent into Dubai. I opened up the window and squinted my eyes from the bright sunlight and the cloudless sky. We were flying over the mountains of Iran. Iran! How crazy is that? Is that even *legal?* I looked at the flight map on the TV screen in front of me, and noticed that the body of water we were about to fly over was labeled as the Arabian Gulf instead of the Persian Gulf. *Interesting*, I thought. *I never knew airlines could get political.*

The Dubai airport reminded me a lot of Las Vegas. It was very shiny with lights and mirrors and sparkly things to marvel over. It didn't take long before I started stressing out over my arrival since Tom and Rebecca would both be at work and couldn't meet me at the airport. Fortunately, they recommended I book an airport concierge service to help me get through immigration and baggage claim. Long story short, after having my fingerprints taken and my retina scanned (yes, this is a thing), locating my electric scooter at baggage claim, and a couple of hiccups with directions and the taxi driver, I made it to Rebecca's campus and got settled.

What followed was the most surreal week of my life. My friends had become pros at playing hosts, so they had my stay well-planned out to work around their class schedules. I rented a manual wheelchair for some outings in case we had to deal with curbs that were a non-starter for my scooter. How a country's royal family can spend billions of dollars building the most expensive city in the world while also creating hundreds of miles of sidewalks with no curb drops or cutouts is beyond me, but we dealt with it. I got to see the view from the 126th floor of the tallest building in the world, the Burj Khalifa. I rolled through two of the world's largest malls, shopped at a glittering souk, had a glamourous Friday brunch at The Atlantis Palm Jumeirah resort, danced in my scooter for three hours at a wine bar-turned nightclub at five o'clock in the afternoon, listened to Sting and Carlos Santana concerts for free from a college campus balcony, and had dinner and drinks with the world's only 7-star hotel (the Burj al-Arab) as a backdrop. I was officially in the photos I had envied so much just a few months earlier.

I could go on and on about the glitz, glamour, and obscene luxury covering every square inch of Dubai, but the most magical moment of my entire trip happened an hour's drive outside of the city, in the desert. During my trip research, I found that a popular activity for tourists was the desert safari. It was a half-day of activity that involved a roller coaster ride of "dune bashing" in four-wheel drive SUVs and a cultural experience at a Bedouin-style camp afterward. Tom called around to see if any of the tour outfitters could accommodate a wheelchair user, and he had success with Orient Tours. The afternoon of our tour (my last full day in Dubai), our driver named Javeed came to pick us up at Tom and Rebecca's campus apartment in a Toyota 4-Runner. He loaded the manual wheelchair in the trunk, Tom loaded me into the SUV's front passenger seat, and we were on our way.

Javeed was very quiet during the one-hour drive out to the dune bashing site. We exchanged small talk and he was pleasant, but otherwise kept mum. Tom and Rebecca told me a bit about the changing landscape as we transitioned from modern city to sand dunes, and after a brief stop to pick up some drinks and snacks, we arrived at the start of the rally, as it were, with about sixteen other SUVs. We had to wait a little while because the drivers had to let air out of all the tires to reduce the pressure to about 15 psi. Because we would be running a very heavy vehicle over soft sand, making the tires slightly flat seemed to help prevent them from spinning into the sand, and thus sinking the vehicle.

Javeed finally got back in the SUV and asked us if we wanted a slow ride or a fast ride. At first I was apprehensive, remembering that Tom had asked me if I was susceptible to motion sickness before he booked the experience (I'm not, thank goodness). Then I looked at Tom and Rebecca, figuring I'd never get a chance to do something like this again. After they nodded, I said fast. No, wait…I said, *FAAAAAAAAST!!!* That was when the 45 miles-per-hour roller coaster ride over the dunes began.

In a word, it was exhilarating! We were sliding sideways, tipping over dune crests, kicking up huge rooster-tail plumes of sand, and wondering the whole time how we never flipped over. It was absolutely incredible. My body was bouncing from side to side, and I was hanging on to every handle within arm's reach. Let's just say that the videos I took weren't the smoothest of my life, but I was hooting and hollering the whole way.

At the end of the rally, all the SUVs gathered at the base of a vast sand dune where everyone got out and began to climb to the top. I, of course, stayed in the SUV and just took some pictures from the passenger seat. Javeed soon returned to our 4-Runner and asked me if I was ready. I looked at him quizzically and asked, "Ready for what?" He replied, "For going to the top of the dune." I burst out laughing and told him he was crazy. Javeed looked at me with a deadly serious expression and said, "Miss Sylvia, today you are going to do what everyone else gets to do. I will make sure of it." I was skeptical, but willing to see where this was going to go.

Javeed called Tom over to the passenger door. Between the two of them, they hoisted me with an arm under each of my legs and my arms across their shoulders, then carried me to the top of the dune. If you've ever tried to climb up a sand dune on your own, you can appreciate the effort this took. The entire way up, I kept thinking, *At least it won't hurt if they drop me!* Once we reached the crest, I was able to stand up by putting an arm over each of their shoulders for support.

I started looking around and just couldn't believe what I was seeing. I was in a Middle Eastern desert, halfway across the world, staring across this enormous expanse of sand dunes as far as the eye could see. Anyone who knows me knows I'm a *huge* Star Wars fan, so I felt like I was on the surface of Tatooine. More importantly, I was gawking at the view, just like everyone else on top of that dune. And just like I would do countless times in my as-yet-unimagined future, I marveled at how I had come to be there, in that wondrous place.

Javeed signaled that we should get going to the Bedouin camp, snapping me out of my reverie. He wanted to get there before everyone else to give me time and the physical space to engage in all the activities before the rest of the crowd arrived. The first thing I saw when we pulled into the camp was several camels waiting for us. There was nothing but sand between our 4-Runner and the camels, but once again, Javeed and Tom came to the rescue. They carried me in the same way they had from the SUV and gently placed me on top of the camel.

Meanwhile, I'm thinking, *I'm sitting on a freakin' camel in the middle of the desert. What is happening right now?!?* I hung on for dear life and managed to keep my seat as the very tall animal stood up and began walking a large slow circle. Once again, I couldn't believe where I was and what I was doing.

Over the next hour and a half, I held a traditional hunting falcon on my arm and got to pet it, ate some dates and drank tea, got a beautiful henna tattoo on my hand and arm, ate a delicious meal, and watched a very entertaining whirling dervish and belly dancing show. Javeed and Tom had to carry me in a plastic chair for a bit to get me between the activities, but there was a paved path between our tented area and a shockingly accessible bathroom.

Soon after night fell, it was time to head back in pitch darkness to the city. We were tired from all the activity and entering food coma territory, so Tom and Rebecca soon fell asleep in the back seat. I was just looking at the beautiful Dubai skyline as we approached the city's outskirts when the up-until-then silent Javeed spoke up. "You remind me of my daughter," he said. This statement caught me off-guard, partly because he was speaking, but mainly because it was so personal. At first, I thought he simply meant that we looked alike, and I was furiously debating how to respond. He saved me the trouble by proceeding to tell me this heartbreaking story.

Javeed is from India. Only 25 percent of Dubai's population is comprised of native Emiratis. The rest consists of temporary foreign workers, mostly from East and South Asian countries like India and the Philippines. Dubai's booming construction and service sectors rely almost entirely on these foreign workers, many of whom financially support family members back in their home countries.

In 2004, one of the largest earthquakes in recorded history hit the Indian Ocean, with an epicenter off Indonesia's coast and a magnitude somewhere around 9.3 on the Richter scale. The resulting tsunamis killed approximately 230,000 people in fourteen countries—including Javeed's sister and her husband in India. Javeed explained that their deaths had made his niece and nephew orphans, so Javeed and his wife took them in as their own children. He and his wife later legally adopted them, so he actually meant his orphaned niece when he referred to his daughter.

Javeed went on to tell me that his daughter had survived polio, and as a result, she was permanently in a wheelchair. He proudly said she wanted to be a doctor, and described her with a smile as *GO GO GO!* all the time. I tried to picture her in my mind. Then Javeed's face went back to a more serious expression. That was why I reminded him of her, he said—as someone who didn't let her disability hold her back from doing anything. He said that, because of me, his mind and heart had been at home in India all day with his family. It took every ounce of strength I had to not break down in tears.

Up until Javeed told me this, I thought he was going out of his way to be kind and help me because it was part of his job, hoping for a good tip (the American way of thinking), or because he was just a nice man. Now I understood that helping me meant something more profound to him—something I could never have imagined had he not said anything to me on the drive back to Dubai. This fleeting moment with a man I hadn't known just a few hours earlier, and would likely never see again, is still one of my fondest travel memories.

But even after that emotional experience, I remain resistant to physical help from others. Why am I so suspicious of the unsolicited kindness of strangers? Is this an American trait, or the result of being part of a vulnerable demographic at the mercy of scammers and predators? I didn't know the root of Javeed's generosity until he told me. How many other people around the world have helped me with deeply personal intentions that I never discovered? For now, I have to find a way to accept that help gracefully without suspecting some ulterior motive, and also acknowledge that I may never know—or *need* to know—the reason behind it.

3 WHO'S AFRAID OF THE BIG RED GORILLA?

It's not every day that you wonder why a big red gorilla wearing a white T-shirt is heading right toward you at the most inopportune moment.

It was a typical London day, which meant it was gray, chilly, and drizzling. I was cold, damp, and exhausted, having spent a very full day exploring Central London. I somehow lucked out for eight hours, with only overcast skies for my visit to the Sky Garden observation deck on the Thames River, the Tate Modern art museum, and Westminster Abbey. However, once I hit the boardwalk along the Thames, that annoying drizzle started. It was just heavy enough that you needed an umbrella, but just windy enough for an umbrella to be impossible.

Still, I decided to adopt the British attitude of keeping a stiff upper lip and getting on with it. Despite the adverse weather, my roll along the Thames on the way to my hotel in the West End yielded several really good photo opportunities.

Unfortunately, in this situation, I didn't have the luxury of time. I hate being in a hurry, but it was 6 PM and the light was fading fast. Mostly for safety reasons, I don't like being out on my own after dark. It makes it harder to navigate in a city I'm not familiar with because the landmarks look different at night. It also makes me more vulnerable as a woman traveling alone in a wheelchair. So, when I approached the beautiful Whitehall Gardens along the Thames, I knew I had to rush to get some good photos.

People ask me all the time how I manage to take photos of myself while positioned nowhere near my cell phone, which I use as my camera. It's not that complicated, but it's a process. I have a relatively small 4-foot travel-sized tripod that comes with a Bluetooth remote shutter. The shutter is a bit smaller than a matchbook, and it's synced up to my cell phone. After I unfold and set up the tripod, I put my cell phone in the holder at the top. Then, I frame the shot using my cell phone camera, take my position, and snap at least a dozen shots in different poses while hiding the little shutter in my hand.

By the time I arrived at the Gardens and started taking out my folding tripod, my fingers were frozen inside my damp gloves. While multiple sclerosis usually has its most damaging effects on my body when it's hot, it does me no favors when my hands are really cold. My fingers become almost nonfunctioning, and it makes even the simplest gesture requiring fine motor skills impossible. So, picture me in this beautiful garden at dusk under overcast skies, freezing cold, wet, *really* pissed off, and struggling to open up this tripod in a big hurry while trying to figure out how I'm going to put a smile on my face for this damn picture.

That was when I saw him.

Out of the corner of my eye, I saw the movement of something totally and irrationally unexpected in the place I was sitting at that very moment. I looked up to see what I assumed was a man lumbering into the garden, wearing a hairy red gorilla suit with a white T-shirt stretched tightly over his torso. He was still about thirty yards away, so I couldn't make out the writing or design on the T-shirt, but I wasn't trying too hard to decipher it. In fact, I was intensely trying not to make any eye contact whatsoever. All I could think was, *Please don't come over here, please don't come over here, please don't come over here…*

Of course, he came over here.

When he approached, I looked up and managed to squeak out what I hoped was a remotely polite sounding hello. I then quickly looked back down and got busy trying to unfold my tripod, hoping this crimson-colored simian would take the hint and go about his evening. He did not. Instead, he uttered the worst possible sentence that anyone could say to me at that particular moment. In a very cheery and decidedly un-posh British accent, he said, "Wow, I wish I had a chair like that to roll around in."

It's hard to overstate the absurdity of things that random strangers say to me or questions they ask when I travel alone. The most common question I get is, "What happened to you?" Why people think they're entitled to know my personal history or private medical information is beyond me. The intent isn't malicious, but it's extraordinarily nosy, borne out of some strange curiosity about wheelchair users. They seem to be particularly curious about me because I'm relatively young and look outwardly healthy. I never tell them the truth about my multiple sclerosis anymore because it always leads to expressions of sorrow or expressions of prayer, neither of which I want or need. I usually have to explain why they shouldn't feel sorry for me because I'm successful, I'm happy, I travel around by myself, blah blah blah. It's *exhausting*.

Then, there are the jokesters who seem to believe they're the first ones to bestow upon me their clever sense of humor. Some examples:

> *Do you have a license for that?*
> *Gee, you're a really good driver!*
> *Don't drink and drive!*
> *Be careful or you'll get a speeding ticket!*
> *Can I get a ride/lift?*
> *Must be nice to be sitting down all day.*
> *You should get a horn or something that goes BEEP BEEP BEEP!*

I promise you, the list goes on and on. How I respond to these statements and questions usually depends on my mood at the moment. I even made T-shirts with several cheeky responses to the "what happened" question because I get it so often. These include:

I got shot by a drug dealer because he didn't like the competition.
I got the wheelchair in a free trial and I forgot to cancel.
I got challenged to a duel and I lost.

These days, my canned response to anyone asking why I'm in a wheelchair is usually just to say that it's personal.

So, on this particularly gray and drizzly and cold London day, I was faced with the decision of how to respond to this seemingly well-meaning red gorilla. Not that it's a good excuse, but I was cold, I was wet, I was tired, and I was frustrated. In other words, I was not my best self. I gave him a look I would describe as more than mildly annoyed and replied, "Wow, I wish I had a pair of working legs that I could walk around in."

I regretted the words as soon as they came out of my mouth, but it was too late. Gorilla Man took a pause. Then he just said, "Yeah…" He might've then muttered something along the lines of "Have a good day!" or goodbye, but I was already back to fiddling with my tripod when he walked away. I finally got everything set up, took my pictures, then rolled back to my hotel as darkness descended upon London.

After a couple of hours, I was warm, dry, and well fed—and notably in a much better mood. I got on my laptop to check my email, and it dawned on me that there may be a media story on this red gorilla. I mean, it's crazy enough that someone might've taken notice of this guy and tried to figure out who he was and why he was wearing that costume. I didn't have to search for very long.

Metro is the United Kingdom's highest circulation print newspaper, and it's published in tabloid format online – similar to the Huffington Post. On October 23, 2019, they published a story titled, "There's a man dressed as a gorilla walking round London all week." *JACKPOT!!!* I started reading, and quickly learned that the man behind the mask was London Metropolitan police officer Tom Harrison. He was walking in a mile-long rectangle every day between 7 AM and 11 PM, covering roughly twenty miles daily on a route that took him past Whitehall—the location of our encounter.

He told the Metro that even though he was a regular runner, walking so many miles every day was a different sort of exercise, and it was taking a toll on his legs, making them feel like lead. He also said it was so interesting interacting with people, some of whom were amused by his crimson getup and others who were even frightened. (This was written before he met me, who was just downright annoyed.)

So, why was this seemingly crazy police officer walking twenty miles a day in a red gorilla suit? My dear reader…he was raising money for charity. He volunteers for the Gorilla Organization, which raises money to protect mountain gorillas in Uganda, Rwanda, and the Congo. Apparently, there had been a huge uncontrolled outbreak of Ebola in the Democratic Republic of Congo, and if mountain gorillas get infected, it's always fatal. He took a week of personal leave from his law enforcement job in Camden to wear a red gorilla suit as a kind of Ebola alert.

After reading all of this, guess who felt like a class-A asshole?

I wasn't sure what to do. I felt like I owed this man an apology, and at the time, I wasn't sure if he would remember me or even how to reach him. Looking back, it was dumb to think that. How many people would forget a woman in a futuristic-looking power wheelchair in Whitehall Gardens speaking so rudely? I'm also sure that given my research and social media skills, I would have found a way to send him a direct message with minimal effort.

In all honesty, I just felt awkward and guilty over the way I responded to him in that moment. This was compounded by my memories of all the other occasions where I responded less than kindly to inquiries or comments from strangers about my existence in a wheelchair. I still stand by the assertion that they're often nosy, inconsiderate, ableist, and sometimes downright rude. But while I can't control how others approach me, I can certainly control how I react to them.

Instead of reaching out to Tom, I donated to his designated charity, the Gorilla Organization. While that doesn't excuse my behavior, it definitely made me feel a little bit better, and I encourage all of you to do the same at www.justgiving.com/gorillaorganization. The experience still makes me think long and hard about how I choose my words in the future when responding to strangers' inquiries. I can't guarantee I won't be a jerk, but please know that I'm continually working on it. And Tom, if you're reading this, I do have a license, I'm a very good driver, I don't drink alcohol, and I'd be happy to give you a lift wherever you need to go.

4 CAN I PRAY FOR YOU?

It's funny how your views about God and religion can change after getting diagnosed with an incurable disease.

I was raised as a Roman Catholic by Cuban-exile parents, so I did all the traditional Catholic things growing up. I was baptized as a baby, had my First Communion, attended CCD (i.e., religious education) classes, etc. After my confirmation, I didn't attend Mass very often because, frankly, it was boring. I was what we call a "cafeteria Catholic," where you more or less pick and choose which aspects of Catholicism you accept and practice. I was also a "C&E" Catholic, which meant I only attended Mass on Christmas and Easter. However, I always wore a crucifix and never really questioned—or took real stock of—my religious faith.

My relationship with religion, especially since becoming a wheelchair user, has become…complicated, and this is the case for many who are newly injured or diagnosed. Some people get angry at God and wonder why they're being punished, especially if they view themselves as faithful and generally good people. Some people look for meaning, believing that their situation is all part of God's plan. Others believe that everything happens for a reason. While some of them find those reasons in familiar places, other people go their whole lives without really understanding why they'll never walk again.

My biggest obstacle to incorporating faith or God or

religion in my life with multiple sclerosis is that I'm an analytical thinker. I look for logic and reason, science and facts, and cause and effect. Nobody knows the real cause of MS. There are some theories out there, but I personally don't meet the generally accepted criteria for a diagnosis. I just happen to be one of several hundreds of thousands of Americans who got the diagnosis between 20 and 40 years old.

Of course, I was emotional after my first presenting symptom. I was terrified, not knowing what my future held. I sobbed, I screamed, my feelings vacillating between sadness and fear. Although I showed no other symptoms typically associated with MS, there was a high probability I would develop it within the next few years. Late in 2002 was when I started the grieving process that is typically associated with such diagnoses. It's possible that I asked, *why me?*

I definitely wasn't angry at God. I've done some pretty stupid things in my life, and I haven't always been the best person. But I don't think I was being punished for some egregious sin or malfeasance or crime against humanity. My family and friends, and my parents especially, did a lot of praying that the diagnosis would never come to pass. When it did, they started praying that I would be okay, that it would progress slowly, or that researchers would find a cure.

I'm sure I said a prayer here or there and asked for something to go well—or at least better—but definitely not with the intensity of people like my mom. I kept going back to the science. I was more comforted by looking at the facts of the disease, and the statistics and studies for the different kinds of available treatments. I looked for things that I could personally manage, instead of relinquishing complete control of my newly diseased body to some spirit in the sky who was supposed to have His way with my life. I don't believe in fate or destiny, but I do understand that there are things that we cannot predict or change. I started treatment right away, and accepted that my body would do whatever it was going to do.

The religiously-themed comments and inquiries from well-wishers started when I bought a walker in 2011, probably because it's pretty apparent that something is out of the ordinary when a woman in her mid-30s is using one. One of the most common questions I get asked as a wheelchair user from total strangers is, *Can I pray for you?* Two of the most common statements are, *God bless you,* or *I will pray for you.*

These requests seem well-intentioned on the surface. However, they're deeply rooted in ableist sentiment that goes largely unrecognized. When most non-disabled people see someone in a wheelchair, many assumptions are often quickly made. People believe we must be in pain, or suffering, or generally unhappy. Most dangerous of all, they think we all want to walk again. Don't get me wrong; some wheelchair users definitely wish they could walk or didn't have whatever condition put them in a wheelchair.

The danger arrives in the notion that we need to be "fixed," and that we're somehow defective or broken because we don't fit the human presumption of "normal." Many people are forced to confront their own fears of potentially becoming disabled when they see us. If they believe they'd never be able to live this way, they think we must be in the midst of a tortured existence. This is where my problem with the contradiction of Christianity comes into play. Weren't people born with disabilities also created in God's image? Wasn't our car accident or diagnosis part of His plan? Why do we need to be "healed" to be accepted by society?

So, when someone mentions praying for me, I usually just nod and say thank you (while internally rolling my eyes)—partly because these sorts of interactions happen in passing, such as in an elevator or waiting in line at the store, but mostly because the root of those prayers makes me angry. But when I had the rare opportunity to really dive into this conversation on a very short cruise to the Bahamas, I went all in.

In late March 2019, I decided to go on a really brief and very low-budget getaway cruise from West Palm Beach to Freeport, Bahamas. There are tons of things that I love about cruising by myself, but a few that I don't. I love to meet new people, and cruises definitely provide the social atmosphere to do that. Depending on the cruise ship, there are also nooks and crannies here and there where you can quietly read a book or get some work done. I especially treasure my solitude during meals, but during this particular lunch, a fellow passenger was having none of it.

It was a glorious spring afternoon at sea, warm but not hot, and not a cloud in the sky. I was on the pool deck where crowds of people were eating, drinking, playing in the pool, or just getting some sun. Lively music was playing, and I was sitting at a table by myself with a Coca-Cola and halfway through my hamburger, scrolling through my phone to keep myself entertained. I didn't think that I looked that open to conversation at that particular moment, but I guess I was wrong.

I was halfway through creating a Facebook post when I looked up and saw him approaching. The dread started creeping into my stomach as this tall and portly man in his mid-fifties made a beeline for my table. He was wearing a sleeveless T-shirt, flip-flops, swim trunks, and a floppy hat. His face was red and he was sweating profusely, but he bore a genuine smile, and his eyes were kind. He introduced himself as Tom as we shook hands, and he sat down—without an invitation, to my mild annoyance, but he seemed nice. He then said he was a minister, and my internal eye-rolling began.

Tom explained that he was on the cruise with his wife, whom he pointed to several tables away, and she waved to me enthusiastically. He said he saw me sitting by the pool the previous evening, enjoying myself while people were dancing. He wanted to talk to me then, but I was having fun. There were also many people around, adding to the fact that the loud music would have precluded any decent conversation. Tom said I had been on his heart since that moment.

I waited for it.

It came.

He asked if he could pray for me.

Given how many times I have been asked this question and how exhausting the whole thing has become, I had to make a decision. I could choose to end the conversation quickly by saying thank you, shaking Tom's hand, and wishing him a great cruise. Or, I could be honest — while remaining polite, of course – and really get to the meat of how I felt about his request.

Because I don't usually get the opportunity to spend a decent amount of time having this conversation with anyone about prayers said in my general direction, I chose the latter.

The first thing I told Tom was not to pray for me, and to save his prayers for someone who really needed them. This response really surprised him. He kind of laughed a little bit, somewhat uncomfortably, and asked me why. I told him I was extremely happy, very successful professionally, and had many supportive family members and friends. I explained to him that I traveled the world by myself in my wheelchair, and was a great mother to my two kids. I had a dependable income and solid medical care. I said I thought it would be best to save his prayers for someone living in poverty or danger or with a terminal illness.

He stopped talking for a minute, and seemed to take a moment to digest what I had said. I took advantage of the silence and asked Tom to confirm that he was a man of God. He was, he said. Now, my assumption with most Christians is that they believe that God has a plan for everyone. Although you can technically pray for whatever you want, God's decision on what happens is final regardless of what you're praying for. I kept my personal feelings about the effectiveness of prayer to myself out of respect for Tom, but I explained this assumption, and he agreed.

Then I asked him the big question: "Have you considered that I'm exactly where God wants me to be, doing exactly what God wants me to be doing?" He looked like I had just hit him over the head with a two-by-four. This was when I started telling Tom about my life's journey.

I told him I was on active duty in the Air Force when I was diagnosed with MS. My symptoms started appearing more rapidly about a month before I was supposed to deploy to Iraq, specifically to a base where we had lost an agent in my organization to a mortar round a few weeks prior. As a result, my deployment was canceled. I will never know, but my MS diagnosis might have saved my life. Becoming a wheelchair user also allowed me to discover compassion and empathy for others that I might never have otherwise. I found a strength within myself that I never knew I had. This strength served me well during a heart-wrenching divorce years later.

Most importantly, because of my travels, I was able to help thousands of other wheelchair users around the world. I told him about my accessible travel writing and travel agency, and explained that over 90 percent of my clients were fellow wheelchair users. I told him about my disability advocacy work. I told him about the scholarship fund that I started to honor my children and provide college assistance for students affected by MS. I would be doing none of this if it wasn't for my diagnosis and my wheelchair.

Tom sat back after hearing all this, smiled gently, and let out a sigh. It seemed to me that he really hadn't considered this perspective before. At that point, I was pretty satisfied with myself, feeling like I had really gotten through to somebody and educated them about something important to me. But that was also the point in our conversation when Tom delivered a huge serving of humble pie to me. "You know what, Sylvia?" he said. "I won't pray for you, as you requested. But I will pray for your ministry instead." That was when I needed to sit back and absorb the enormity of what *he* said.

Having grown up Catholic, I have always had an idea in my mind of what a ministry is. Generally speaking, these are church members, priests, pastors, missionaries, etc., who group together to attend to the needy. In simple biblical terms, it means to serve on God's behalf. To be entirely upfront, I never felt called by God to do what I do. Much of my travel feels like a purely selfish endeavor, almost like one endless vacation. I have found a way to monetize my travel expertise as a travel agent. Still, I get only a modest amount in ad revenue writing for my blog. That, I do as a service to the wheelchair community, and it's fun. If it wasn't fun, I wouldn't be doing it. But I never thought about it in terms of being a ministry. I felt truly humbled by his perspective, despite his religious faith being orders of magnitude greater than mine.

So, now what? I told Tom I had never thought of my advocacy work as a ministry, and he patiently and thoughtfully explained the many ways it was. Now *I* was the one sitting back and gently smiling, listening to this minister who was a total stranger just moments earlier share his passion and belief with me—an ardent non-believer. The guilt started to descend on my heart. I had been so ready to quickly dismiss this well-meaning man with a brusque word of thanks and barely hidden resentment.

What will I do the next time someone offers up prayers that I don't want or need? Chances are I won't be in a situation to have a lengthier conversation like I had with Minister Tom. My feelings about prayer still haven't changed, and Tom may still want me to be healed. However, I've realized that it hurts no one to change my own perspective on accepting those prayers with more humility. Yes, I am still *really* frustrated with the contradiction and ableism inherent in prayers for me to be somehow converted to "normal." However, I will have other opportunities to more gently explain why we don't need to be fixed.

I needed to get back to my lunch, so I thanked Tom with great sincerity and told him that I would appreciate his prayers for my ministry very much. I told him it was such a pleasure to chat with him, and that I hoped he and his wife enjoyed the rest of their cruise. This time, I really meant it.

5 I. AM. BATMAN.

I love seeing and meeting and talking with other wheelchair users in foreign countries—except when they're *super* creepy.

I mean, it may sound weird at first, but it's human nature to want to be around people who are like us. I'm a fluent Spanish speaker, and when I'm visiting a country where Spanish is nowhere close to sounding like the local language, my ears always perk up when I hear tourists speaking it. I love to approach them, say hello in Spanish, then find out what country they're from. God forbid they're also Cuban, because the conversation is definitely going to get boisterous! When I visited Shanghai, there were almost no Western tourists there, let alone Americans. I probably got a little too excited when I ran into three Americans from Chicago in the Shanghai World Financial Center lobby.

I run into some pretty cool wheelchair and scooter users during my travels, both on cruises and land trips. I started using my current power wheelchair in October 2018, and because it looks so unique and futuristic, I get a lot of questions about it from other "wheelies." I love that it's such positive conversation starter, as opposed to the awkward, *So, what do* you *have going on [that you're also in a chair]?*

In November 2018, I met a lovely older gentleman in Gibraltar who was in a beat-up manual chair. He was fascinated with my Whill Ci power chair, and we talked a lot about his interesting background. In April 2019, I met a wonderful man in

Cuba who is a double amputee. I was heartbroken to see his manual chair, as it was a reach to call it anything close to being an adequate mobility aid. It's not legal for American tourists to give cash to people on the street, even though he had a hat with a few coins in it. We spoke for several minutes, and afterward I gave him 10 CUC, which is roughly the equivalent of US$10. I wanted to give him so much more, but I was afraid he would get in trouble for possessing half a month's worth of the average Cuban's income. Just that modest amount could feed him (or someone else) for weeks.

It's tempting to seek out fellow members of your "people" abroad and assume that you automatically have something in common. That group could be anything, depending on where you are. It could be fellow Americans, people of the same race or gender identity or sexual orientation, people who speak your language, or in my case, fellow wheelchair users. I know that wheelchair users aren't all the same, and it's an annoying stereotype that members of any marginalized group all somehow magically know each other.

None of these facts diminished my enthusiasm when I saw a power wheelchair user in the beautiful main square of Ljubljana, the capital of Slovenia. I had never heard of the former Yugoslavian republic's capital city until I read a magazine article about its great wheelchair accessibility, and I'm so glad I visited essentially on a whim. Slovenia fared much better economically than other former Yugoslavian states like Bosnia and Croatia, and it shows in the standard of living. While not a tourism juggernaut as big as Croatia, which has the advantage of multiple cruise ship ports and *Game of Thrones* filming locations, Slovenia has stunning destinations like Lake Bled and the Vogel ski resort. Ljubljana has also become a mecca for foodies and wine lovers, with a regular Friday food market that is a must-see for visitors.

The first time I saw him, I was with my tour guide, Miha. I saw him from a distance, so I could only tell that he was wearing all black and using a large black power chair. Miha said he was there pretty much every day and never seemed to bother anybody. I filed that away somewhere in my head and went on my way exploring the city.

Two days later, I had the whole day to myself to explore Ljubljana. Around sunset, I found myself in the main square again, along with the mysterious power wheelchair user. This time, he noticed me first and decided to approach. As he neared, I was able to see up close who I was dealing with. He was dressed exactly the same as two days prior, in a long-sleeved T-shirt, black pants, black boots, black fingerless gloves, and a black wool beanie. He had long black hair, a long black beard, and black-rimmed eyeglasses. His all-black chair had definitely seen better days. He was eating corn on the cob, and he smelled like peanut butter.

In excellent English, Mr. Black Everything said hello and asked me for my name. He introduced himself as Batman and offered me some of his corn on the cob. I politely declined. That was when things got weird.

He started by asking me typical questions, like where I lived, why I was in Ljubljana, etc. Then he asked me if I was single. Of course, I made the mistake of replying that I was. Quickly realizing that mistake, I threw in there that I was divorced and had two kids, as if that would derail him from wherever he was going. It did not.

Batman told me I would feel right at home in his basement.

Batman said he had some great restraints that would keep me from escaping.

Batman said it would be a lot of fun to tie me up.

Batman smiled and said that once he had me, I wouldn't want to get away.

You're probably wondering what I was thinking, or better yet, how I was replying during this entire exchange, if you want to call it that. I'm usually quick on my feet, so to speak, when it comes to conversation. But when somebody says things to me that are so completely shocking and unexpected, even I can be prone to speechless moments.

In the midst of me trying to figure out what to say and how to say it, Batman reached down over my right rear wheel and flicked the little yellow lever that puts my scooter in neutral. How he knew where to find that lever, or that flipping it would achieve his desired effect of rendering me immobile, is beyond me. I now had to turn my scooter off, flip the lever back, and turn my scooter back on so that I could move.

I want to be perfectly clear that at no point during this "conversation" with Batman did I feel physically threatened or unsafe. We were in a public and bustling square with tons of people around, and while he clearly had some physical ability, there was nothing that he could really do to hurt me. I mean, his chair might have been faster than mine, and it actually would have been somewhat comical to see him try to chase me in my scooter.

While I wasn't worried about falling prey to Batman, I had unfortunately fallen prey to one of the more misogynistic expectations of women these days—the requirement to smile and be polite, no matter what is being said to you. With few exceptions, I am polite to a fault with strangers. Here is a guy who is making some alarming statements about what he wants to do with me in his basement, and I'm just nodding my head and saying things like *Wow*, and *Okayyyy*, and *I don't think so…*, instead of the more appropriate, *Get the fuck away from me, you fucking weirdo!* In the end, we're all Monday morning quarterbacks.

This incident really made me think about a couple of important issues surrounding solo travel, especially when you're a woman. The first is the self-imposed pressure I feel to be a positive representative of the United States. No, I am not an appointed ambassador, and I don't get paid to make America look good. However, in every country I visit, I am bound and determined not to be *that American*. I want to be polite and respectful to everyone I interact with. I want to learn at least a few words of the language. I want to leave the locals I meet with the ability to say, *Hey, I met this American woman today, and she was really cool.* I was walking a fine line between not being an asshole and making sure this wannabe superhero-on-wheels didn't think I was remotely interested in seeing his Batcave.

The second issue I'm always concerned with is my personal safety. All women who travel solo have to worry about this. No matter how physically strong or fast we might be, we're typically seen as easy targets, especially in countries with cultures where men dominate society. In my twenties, I was a fit and healthy Air Force officer and a Special Agent. I didn't know any martial arts moves, but I was practiced in some basic defensive tactics that would've at least allowed me to get out of a bad situation and run for help. As a woman in a wheelchair, that's not an option.

As a result, when I travel abroad, I have some pretty strict rules that I lift only on rare occasions. I'm always around other people. I'm back in my hotel room by nightfall unless I'm taking photos or attending an event. If I'm rolling back to my hotel after dark, I always try to be close to other people (without making them think I'm some creepy stalker). That way, if someone approaches me, there will be somebody close enough to hear me yell. I try hard to stay away from drunk people because personal experience tells me they love to lean on me and my chair, especially in crowds. I also recently started carrying a personal alarm.

After taking furious stock of the current situation, I determined I wasn't in any danger. *Yeah. I can take him.* Even so, it all reminded me that I can't—and shouldn't—make assumptions about anyone when it comes to my safety abroad. Someone who appears to be harmless could be thinking (whether seriously or not) about ways to hurt or otherwise take advantage of me, and people who look dangerous can turn out to be my fiercest protectors. I'm reminded that I have to be on top of my security game in every situation, and pay attention to even the smallest red flags. However, I also need to be open to genuine kindness, and allow myself to give people the benefit of the doubt. It's a tricky balancing act.

I finally snapped out of it and looked at my watch, vaguely telling Batman I had somewhere indeterminate I really needed to be. After a long look, he bid me farewell with a warning that I would miss him and later regret my decision to leave. *Sorry to break it to you, Batman, but I'm glad I left when I did. However, I can sometimes still smell that nasty peanut butter when I think of you.*

6 THE TROUBLE WITH MAGGIE

Nothing spells trouble like a pub filled with men of the Royal Air Force drinking copious amounts of alcohol.

Before I get into the details of this beer-fueled tale, there are two things you should know about my social behavior when I travel by myself. First, with extremely few exceptions (like photos, concerts, or meeting friends), I never go out at night in a new city. I guarantee you that a woman traveling alone in a wheelchair has no business being in a foreign bar at night where no one knows her, or English for that matter. This is primarily for safety reasons, but mainly because by 7 PM, I'm completely exhausted. I usually get an early start to make the most of daylight and smaller crowds for photography. Then I go on tours or navigate the sights almost nonstop until sundown. I either grab a quick dinner very close to my hotel or order room service before taking a hot shower and getting comfortable in my pajamas. This is my idea of heaven.

Second, you should know that meeting men in a romantic capacity figures absolutely nowhere in my travel plans. The only time I ever bring makeup or even dresses on a trip is when I go on a cruise, and even then, I often choose to skip formal nights unless I'm cruising with the aforementioned best friend.

There are a couple of reasons why men aren't on my travel radar. I'm totally and completely single, and totally and completely interested in attractive and intelligent men. However, when I'm traveling, I'm busy. Like, *I really don't want to be distracted from what I'm doing and seeing and learning* busy. If I'm not on a private tour with a guide, I'm usually wandering around a museum, or garden, or downtown area where you don't just bump into single men and start a profound or flirtatious conversation. And as you already know, I don't frequent bars by myself—which would be especially weird since I don't drink alcohol anymore.

I also generally don't interact with men when I travel because, like it or not, being in a wheelchair tends to be off-putting to potential dates. Look, it is what it is, and I get it. When you're single and carefree and traveling, you're most likely looking for a temporary hook-up and not someone who you really need to get to know before moving further. I fall into the second category. I believe that I'm physically attractive, but it's simply easier to pass me up for a more "standard" female version when you're just passing through. I come with a specific set of instructions, whereas a woman traveling in heels simply needs a sticker that says LIFT HERE.

These two rules go out the window, however, when I'm traveling with my best friend. Erin thinks I have no business *not* going out at night in a new city, wheelchair or not. While most of my traveling is solo, Erin and I take a big "bestie" trip once a year. She mostly lets me pick a destination due to my accessibility needs, and I take it as an opportunity to visit places that are otherwise difficult to navigate by myself as a wheelchair user. This particular trip was a combination of Madrid, Gibraltar, and Tangier.

We started with several days in Madrid, which was gorgeous despite rainy weather, and the food was incredible! We even took a day trip out to Segovia to see the Royal Palace of La Granja, the Alcázar, and the Segovia Cathedral. From Madrid, we had quite the unplanned 9-hour adventure of getting to Gibraltar through a combination of two trains, two taxis, and three buses because heavy storms had recently washed out large sections of track. We had an epic day trip by ferry from Tarifa in Spain to Tangier, Morocco, which was my first visit to Africa and one of the best travel experiences of my life. Then we spent two more days exploring the fascinating history of the British overseas territory of Gibraltar.

Sadly, our epic vacation was coming to a close on a Monday. The next day we had to head back to Madrid by bus and train to catch a flight back to Miami on Wednesday morning. I was utterly exhausted after a full day of sightseeing and not getting much sleep the night before, and more than willing to follow my traveling rules and go to bed early. However, Erin had circled something in red on our virtual calendar the second we arrived in Gibraltar: karaoke. She had seen a chalkboard A-sign outside an English pub in Gibraltar's main square indicating there would be karaoke on Monday night. Participation was not optional or up for discussion.

You have to understand that Erin is an even bigger fool for karaoke than I am. I have a good voice, but Erin has sung the National Anthem at NFL football games. She knows what she's doing. I knew that if there were a karaoke night in Gibraltar during our stay, she would find it, and we would inevitably find ourselves there.

When we first arrived around 8 PM at All's Well, a pub in Casemates Square frequented mostly by locals, it was pretty empty. It seemed karaoke was running a bit late, so Erin and I headed to a restaurant next door to grab a quick dinner. By the time we returned to the pub an hour later, the scene had changed entirely. Karaoke was in full swing, as was the drinking and revelry by no less than a baker's dozen of very handsome British men— many of whom were actually singing.

Now, any karaoke veteran can tell you that this is an aberration. Don't get me wrong; both men and women thoroughly enjoy karaoke. In Asian countries, karaoke is almost a religion for male executives. However, in Western countries, you are far more likely to find a large group of women at a karaoke bar being drunk and silly for something like a bachelorette party. Erin and I were thoroughly ready to find out what this was all about.

Finding a place where the two of us could sit comfortably was awkward. A table where a chair can be removed is the best for me because I can just roll up in my power chair. However, all of those tables were in the back of the bar. The seats closest to the stage, where karaoke was going on, were at tables with benches. I managed to awkwardly park close to one of the benches so Erin could sit next to me while leaving enough space for people to get to and from the stage.

After getting a drink, Erin's first mission was to find out who these lovely men were. It didn't take her long to discover that they were all in the Royal Air Force and in town for a week of training. It also didn't take her long to let them know that she was an Air Force reservist and I was an Air Force veteran. Americans, of course. Within minutes, we were the talk of the bar, and soon had something of an audience of that baker's dozen around our little table and benches. It didn't hurt that we were the only women there either, if you don't count the drunk 50 year-old wearing cut-off shorts, a ripped t-shirt, and dancing by herself.

Erin was not romantically available at the time, and I didn't consider myself to be a viable flirtation partner for any of the men in the bar that night. I was dressed very casually and not wearing a spot of makeup, so we were only putting out friendly (i.e., platonic) vibes. I was also the only sober person in the joint, sadly out of necessity. When drinking requires you to use the bathroom frequently and there are no accessible toilets nearby, you tend to curtail or altogether nix your alcohol consumption. Unfortunately, being sober deprives you of that oh-so-very-attractive boost of confidence that comes with being tipsy, so I resigned myself to watching everybody else get silly and enjoying a bit of karaoke in the process.

Until Craig started flirting with me.

You should understand that I'm dumber than a box of rocks these days when it comes to accepting looks or signals of attraction from men. This is all utterly due to being in a wheelchair. Before I got married in 2004, I was a huge flirt and never really had a boyfriend for longer than a few months at a time. My confidence was through the roof, and if I wanted a man, I usually got him. But now as a divorcée, I'm 99.9 percent sure that if an attractive man looks and smiles at me as he walks past, he's just being polite and isn't doing so because he thinks I'm pretty. It's hard to think otherwise when most people in public stare at you solely because of the wheelchair and not in spite of it.

After explaining this to you, you're probably wondering how I know that Craig was flirting with me. Our conversation started typically enough. He's a Royal Air Force officer, so it was easy to talk about our jobs, life in the military, training, travel, etc. It was also hard to talk about anything more profound than that because it was deafening in that bar. We were also moving between the table and the stage to sing, and everybody else was shuttling between the table and the bar to drink more.

As the night progressed, when Craig and I did talk, we were physically closer to each other with each snippet of conversation. He would touch my hand. I would touch his face when talking into his ear. While dancing and singing to karaoke, he would come over and hug or kiss me on the cheek or hold my hands. For the first time in a while, I got those butterflies that everybody talks about. I mean, here I was, wearing a plain black sweater and plain black leggings with no makeup on, *in a wheelchair*, and this super-hot Royal Air Force officer was totally into me! I was absolutely in heaven...until Maggie showed up.

The time was approximately 12:30 AM. I originally wanted to leave no later than 11 PM so Erin and I could take the night's last accessible taxi back to our hotel since we had to wake up early the next morning to catch a bus. If we stayed any later, we would have to walk/roll twenty minutes — all uphill — back to our hotel in the middle of the night in a totally unfamiliar place. However, it wasn't that difficult for Erin to convince me to stay since we were both having so much fun, and she said she didn't mind the walk. The gorgeous Craig was being super flirty and very touchy-feely, and I was enjoying every second of the attention.

Maggie appeared in the form of a song by Rod Stewart. Craig was the singer, so he got up on stage with a few other people who were just dancing and enjoying the song. Everyone was absolutely shit-faced, or pissed as the British locals like to say. Craig was a decent singer, and he seemed to be happy enough singing the song. *Maggie, I couldn't have tried anymore...*

Right after the song ended, he came straight over to me with a slight wobble. He put both arms on my shoulders after running his hands through my hair. Then he put his mouth right next to my ear after kissing me on the cheek. I was *very* eager to hear what he had to say. "That song makes me so sad," he slurred. "It reminds me of my wife's mother, and she just died."

As a public service announcement, I will now inform you that the quickest way to completely turn a woman off and kill her lady boner is to tell her that your mother-in-law just passed away, and in the process, disclose to her that you're married.

Everything (for me, anyway) went downhill pretty quickly after that. Craig went from really tipsy to completely drunk within a few minutes, and he promptly left the bar for his hotel with only a wave to everyone. Still being the only sober one in the bar and now having no one left to talk to or flirt with, for the next thirty minutes I felt really alone in a room filled with people having a great time. We closed up the bar at 1 AM, and Erin and I started the long walk/roll in the cold back to our hotel. I went to bed feeling nothing but disappointment, and no small amount of discouragement.

However, I was buoyed the next day by looking through the photos and videos I took the night before. It turned out Craig wasn't the only guy in the bar that night who flirted with me. He's the one I clicked with the most, but there were plenty of other airmen who were super attractive and seemed to think the same of me. Maybe the alcohol contributed a little bit, but I'd like to believe it was the energy and self-confidence I was putting out more than any chemical enhancement. It sounds weird, but not caring as much about your appearance and caring more about having fun and interacting positively with other people can be *very* attractive—even more so than typical good looks.

Nothing physical was going to happen with Craig that night anyway, even if he hadn't been married. But just the slight touches, the nudges, the lightning-quick caresses, and the looks that linger a second too long...*those* are the things that remind us we're human and need that human connection, no matter how much someone like me says it's not a necessary part of our lifestyle. It reminded me that I was still capable of waking up those butterflies, wheelchair and all. When I look at those photos now, I don't feel disappointed at all. I just smile and say to myself, *Gurrrrllll...you still got it.* And Maggie can suck it.

7 WHAT ARE YOU LOOKING AT?

I've gotten used to totally random strangers staring at me as a healthy-looking wheelchair-using curiosity, but some Chinese people take it to a whole new level.

If you've traveled to any major world city in the last five years, you have no doubt seen or come in contact with a large group of Chinese tourists. This is because China's middle class is growing by leaps and bounds, so they have more disposable income for travel. Tourists from mainland China (as opposed to Hong Kong; more on that later) now comprise one of the largest percentages of global travelers. For example, I came across an interesting situation during a road trip through Montana, Idaho, and Wyoming in 2016. I was staying at a hotel in West Yellowstone, just outside one of the main entrances for the national park. Apparently, a large group of Chinese tourists was also staying there. Their presence was frequent enough that the placards for every breakfast item were typed in both English and in Mandarin. I spend over 130 nights every year in hotels outside of Asia, and I had never seen this.

I soon found myself running into these sizeable Chinese tour groups everywhere I went. Vienna. Sydney. Frankfurt. Auckland. Munich. Madrid. Dublin. Every time I got near the group in my electric scooter (which was my mobility aid at the time), the stares and the pointing would commence. On the few occasions where I found myself physically surrounded by one of these groups inside a museum or other attraction, I was reminded that the Chinese concept of personal space is extremely different from the American concept—as in, nonexistent. They also had zero regard, respect, or deference for wheelchair users, constantly cutting in front of me, leaning on me, or pushing me when they wanted to see something. Seeing them through my American lens, I didn't understand their behavior.

I remember the first encounter I had in my electric scooter with a large group of Chinese mainlanders. I was in Australia's Blue Mountains, about two hours outside of Sydney, in November 2016. I was on an accessible day trip, and on my way from a gift shop to my tour guide's accessible van, I passed a large tour bus surrounded by roughly fifty Chinese tourists. I was hard to miss in my bright red scooter, so as soon as I approached, I had fifty pairs of eyes glued to my wheels. I felt like I was in one of those dreams where you're wandering around completely naked.

This was unnerving at the time because I didn't understand what the big deal was. Surely in a country with over a billion people, at least *some* were using wheelchairs or scooters, right? The really creepy part is, they didn't even say anything. Sometimes the men would point at me. Sometimes, the women would whisper something to each other as they stared. Most of them looked upset. Or disturbed. Or confused. Knowing very little about Chinese culture at the time, I had no idea why, and even less of an idea of how to read their body language. Was I wearing an offensive color? Did I have something upsetting stuck to my clothing or scooter? I was gripped by insecurity, panicking that I was doing something wrong. This situation would continue to chase me through over a dozen countries in the following year.

In late 2017, I decided to visit Hong Kong the following February as part of a three-week Asia tour, including stops in New Zealand and Singapore. Hong Kong was the last stop of the three, and to say I was apprehensive is an understatement because I assumed the staring would be nonstop. It would be my first visit to China proper, and despite the fact that Hong Kong is politically separate from mainland China, I was still going to be in the cultural (and physical) minority. I should note that the Chinese in

Hong Kong are different than those on the mainland. It's hard to concisely explain why, but they just are. Both Hong Kong Chinese (the socially middle rung) and Singapore Chinese (the elite top rung) tend to look down on mainlanders the same way that American city dwellers in the northeast might look down on rural residents in the southeast. I was hoping this might make the staring and pointing situation better, and at first, it did—until it didn't.

During my second day in Hong Kong, I decided to visit the Hong Kong Natural History Museum. The accessibility was quite good, and the exhibit signs were all in English and Chinese, so I could understand everything I was looking at. It really was an excellent museum, and I was in a good mood as I was exiting the last exhibit.

I started rolling in my scooter across the large entrance hall on my way to the gift shop when I noticed a Chinese man headed in the same direction on my right. He was probably in his late 30s, tall and thin, and walking at a very brisk pace. I heard him start mumbling in Chinese in my blind spot before seeing him out of the corner of my right eye. As he got to roughly my two o'clock position, he looked at me over his left shoulder. He gave me the dirtiest look I've ever received in my life, uttered what sounded like a Chinese curse word, spit on the ground in my general direction, and kept walking. It was one of the rare moments in my life where I was utterly speechless.

To be perfectly fair, out of the thousands of Chinese people I had come across during my travels, none of them had ever given me such a vile look as this man. Maybe he got fired that morning. Maybe his girlfriend broke up with him. Who knows? However, the incident really shook me. I just didn't understand what was so wrong with me as a person in a public space, just because I couldn't walk.

Later that night, I had scheduled a walking tour of "Kowloon at Night" with a fantastic tour guide named Olivia. She had grown up in the United States and spoke flawless English, but returned to her family's native China to be a tour guide. You haven't experienced Hong Kong until you've been to Kowloon after dark. The Temple Street market is one of the most popular tourist attractions, and with good reason. It's a living and breathing entity with people constantly moving. Sweaty men are rolling dollies and carts back and forth filled with fruits and vegetables and merchandise. Locals were singing karaoke in outdoor tents, and the noise from competing singers performing just a few yards from each other in neighboring tents was deafening. The lighted signs everywhere were blinding. It was overwhelming and utterly fantastic.

During one of our tour's quieter moments when we were standing in front of the Tin Hau temple complex, I told Olivia about my incident at the museum. She just rolled her eyes, then said she was really sorry that had happened to me. Unfortunately, she said it was all too common. She explained that many Chinese in Hong Kong are practitioners of Taoism, one of the common Asian religions. She noted that many Taoists believe that people in wheelchairs or with physical disabilities or deformities are being punished in their current life for sins they committed in a past life. Suddenly, understanding dawned. I was on the receiving end of centuries of belief, perception, and misunderstanding of people with disabilities.

As for the pointing and the staring that didn't necessarily involve any dirty looks (or spitting), she said that behavior was often out of curiosity. Generally speaking, the Chinese, and many Asian families overall, tend to hide their wheelchair users. People with disabilities in the Asian culture are often considered a source of shame to the family. They aren't particularly welcomed by society, thus not frequently seen in public. That's why the only wheelchair users you'll typically see in China are senior citizens. They're almost expected to be in wheelchairs once they reach a certain age, and are highly respected for their seniority. You will also always see them in *manual* wheelchairs (typically the older metal hospital style), being pushed by a family member.

Having this newfound understanding, someone might have called me crazy for deciding to visit Shanghai (a.k.a. the belly of the beast) in April 2019. The idea all started because I found a ridiculous flight deal on one of my iPhone travel apps, and I couldn't pass it up. However, I think there was this subconscious voice telling me I needed to challenge my assumptions, and *really* confront the challenge of a culture that (presumably) viewed me negatively. So, I booked my flights with a one-night stopover in Los Angeles in each direction, and booked six nights at a hotel in downtown Shanghai near a major pedestrian shopping area. I love big cities, and Shanghai is the largest city in all of China. I was intimidated, but fortunately, I found a tour company that would help me explore despite their services not being fully accessible.

After only three hours of sleep, thanks to a very delayed flight, my first day in Shanghai involved a day trip to a local water town called Zhujiajiao. Water towns acquired this name because they are crisscrossed with canals, like Chinese versions of Venice. The sidewalks that lined the canals were bumpy but passable. I loved that everyone in this town was local Chinese, without an American or European tourist in sight. The shops were small, and while some contained trinkets and souvenirs, most sold locally-made goods and aromatic regional foods. While I was happily rolling down one of these narrow alleys with my tour guide, it happened the first time.

I noticed a short and stocky Chinese man wearing a striped shirt and a hat, walking about ten feet in front of me at my one o'clock position. The Chinese *love* to take photos even more than Americans, so I wasn't surprised to see him holding a selfie stick with his phone at the end of it. Except…the front-facing camera on the phone wasn't pointed at him; it was pointed at me. He was trying to take a picture of me without me realizing it.

You might think I was annoyed, or upset, or creeped out. But oddly enough, it was quite the opposite. My tour guide greeted him in a very gentle and friendly fashion and asked if she could help him with something. Apparently, the man was trying to take a picture of me because he thought my relatively new futuristic-looking power wheelchair was one of the coolest things he had ever seen. At least, that's what my tour guide said while translating his words. He started smiling sheepishly and told her that he was too embarrassed to ask if he could take a picture of me (thus, the subterfuge). I was so flattered and told him to go ahead because, at that point, I realized that I was no longer a freak in China — I was a *rock star*.

Over the next five days in Shanghai, I had no less than ten people *every single day* asking if they could take a picture of my chair or a selfie of themselves with me and my chair. Dozens of locals would approach my tour guides (or strangers near me who spoke English) and ask them to ask me where I got my chair, how much I paid for it, and where they could buy one. After a few days of this, I realized that the only wheelchairs I had seen were old manual ones, and all were being used by elderly locals.

The truth is, the average Chinese person can't buy an electric scooter or power wheelchair in China. My über-modern power chair is a source of curiosity and mild admiration in the United States. But in Shanghai, it left people downright awestruck. Men would follow me or walk alongside me just staring at my chair, not saying anything for a long time. I promise you, this is not as creepy as it sounds. I quickly learned that by smiling, waving, and saying *Ni hao!* (hello in Mandarin), those serious looks of consternation I had seen in so many Chinese tour groups around the world would very quickly turn to bright smiles and laughter. I had broken down this huge cultural wall with just my power wheelchair, a smile, and one little word.

Little did I know that my best experience in China was yet to come. On my fourth day in Shanghai, I went on another day trip with a tour guide to a much larger water town about two hours away called Suzhou. This is a UNESCO World Heritage Site, and the city is absolutely stunning. It's a fascinating blend of modern buildings and ancient traditional Chinese architecture, and the waterways are crisscrossed with beautiful bridges filled with colorful flowers.

When we arrived, the first thing we did was to visit one of the largest botanical gardens in China. I found a shady spot to wait in while my tour guide went to pick up our entrance passes. While I was waiting, I noticed a group of about ten Chinese college students out of the corner of my eye. I quickly glanced over at them, and they were all looking back at me, smiling sheepishly. Some of them whispered to each other, looking very apprehensive. I motioned for them to approach, then tried to see if any of them spoke English. Most mainland Chinese don't speak any English because, honestly, they really don't have to. Unless they work in the tourism industry or the financial sector, they don't need it.

After a bit of back-and-forth discussion among themselves, one young woman finally approached me. She spoke *maybe* a few words of English, but with that and a few hand signals, we could communicate a little bit about my name and where I was from. My tour guide finally returned, and she was able to start translating for us. The group found me to be a source of fascination—this smiling American woman wearing Chuck Taylors, by herself in her cool-looking power wheelchair in the middle of Suzhou.

My guide explained to them who I was, what I did for a living, and why I was visiting Shanghai. Several of the young women told my guide to say to me that they thought I was amazing, and one of them said I was her hero (I'm rapidly fanning my face with my hands at this point). In very broken English, one of the young men managed to tell me that he thought I was beautiful (like, I'm *swooning*). One by one, I learned and tried to pronounce their names in Mandarin, much to the amusement of everyone present. I asked what they were studying and what they wanted to do after they graduated, knowing full well this was still China and lamenting that their dreams may never come to pass by the sheer realities of living under communist rule.

Even though the language was a barrier, technology definitely was not. Once they found out I had the WeChat app on my phone — basically, the only communications app that isn't blocked or censored in China — they all wanted to connect with me. Thanks to a QR code that can easily be scanned, I had ten new Chinese "friends" within twenty seconds. I'm sure that Customs and Border Protection would be thrilled to see that on my phone at LAX a few days later.

These young, bright, and cheerful kids were all smiles when we parted ways, and were so incredibly flattered when I was able to say thank you and goodbye to them in Mandarin. It was yet another inspiring and fleeting moment in my travels, but it really triggered some massive introspection. *How long does it really take to get an accurate picture of an entire culture? And is it up to them to show us who they are, or up to us to look for it and see it?*

There's a lot of debate in professional travel circles about the difference between being a tourist and a traveler. The tourist visits different places, usually for short periods, to see and do. The traveler visits different places to know and *experience*. I honestly don't think that you can truly understand a foreign culture without living in that country for an extended time. I have many "digital nomad" friends who can live and work abroad for months on end, but that lifestyle is just not in the cards for me. So, is it even possible to be a traveler instead of a tourist during a shorter stay? Was my enlightening experience with the Chinese people a fluke, or was it something I could actively initiate during future travels?

I have found that the only way to really get to know at least the outskirts of a foreign people is to, well…talk to them. And I'm not talking about asking for directions or a passerby to take a photo of you. Find out where *they* eat and where they go to relax on weekends. Ask them what it's like to live in their country and how kids grow up there. If you see something you don't understand, ask a local about it. Don't get me wrong; I have learned more things than I could ever hope to remember from some pretty fantastic tour guides. Just don't be afraid to smile and wave to someone who happens to be looking at you—or yes, even staring. There's a good chance they may be just as curious about you as you are about them. There's also a good chance you'll learn something you didn't know an hour ago, and maybe make some new friends along the way—even if Customs asks you about them at the airport.

8 DOWN FOR REPAIRS

Wheelchair users are not only experts at planning; we're experts at not losing our shit and quickly adapting when absolutely everything goes sideways.

I've known this ever since I started using a wheelchair full-time in 2014, but for some crazy reason, that didn't stop me on this cold and blustery day in Berlin, Germany. I had already spent five full days in the capital city, and had utterly exhausted my to-do and must-see lists. Most normal people would just take the blank date on the itinerary and relax—go for a stroll, have some drinks, people watch, and maybe buy some last-minute souvenirs. Not this overachiever. I was going to squeeze every last drop out of Berlin.

The first thing I have to figure out while researching a destination is if there are any wheelchair accessible things to do or see. If nothing is waiting for me, then why would I bother to go? Next, I have to determine if wheelchair accessible transportation exists. This isn't always a guarantee, and can include accessible taxis and accessible public transportation. Hotels can also be tricky because accessibility standards aren't uniform globally, and I've arrived at more than one hotel to find out it wasn't truly accessible. Even if I achieve this trifecta of accessible transportation, lodging, and attractions, there's still the matter of the destination itself. The sidewalks might be in bad shape, for example, and there may be very few curb cuts at intersections. People might not be very nice towards people with disabilities, or there may be nowhere for me to eat if the restaurants aren't accessible. Figuring all of this out can take dozens of research hours and doesn't create much space for spontaneity. It also doesn't mean those carefully crafted plans can't fall apart on a dime like a house of cards.

So, here I am, on a Thursday night at 10 PM in my Berlin hotel room, trying to figure out what to do the following day before I fly home on Saturday. I'm looking on Google Maps for nearby cities that might be intriguing options for a day trip. At this point, I'm not exactly sure how I'm going to get to some places, but as I mentioned above, priority number one is finding a cool destination with accessible things to see and do. I also don't have to worry about a hotel room. Based on this cursory initial research, Potsdam fit the bill.

Intended to be a "picturesque, pastoral dream," Potsdam is situated on the Havel River. The city was the residence of Prussian kings and the German Kaiser until 1918. It includes two palaces: The Sanssouci Palace, which is the largest UNESCO World Heritage Site in Germany; and the Cecilienhof Palace, where Churchill, Truman, and Stalin met in 1945 to decide how to administer post-war Germany.

Now that I was getting excited about what Potsdam had to offer, I had to figure out how to get there. Fortunately, that part turned out to be easy. One of the lines on Berlin's robust metro system went directly from Potsdam to a station close to my hotel. *Easy peasy, lemon squeezie!* There were accessible bus options from there that would help me see the city and avoid draining my power chair's battery. I was all set after only ninety minutes of planning, which is about as spontaneous as I could possibly get.

I woke up at 6 AM the following morning to catch one of the first trains out of Berlin to Potsdam. I didn't get much sleep the night before because I was so excited! The morning was cold, but I bundled up the best I could, and I knew that the day would slowly warm up when the sun was due to peek out a few hours later.

I boarded the S-bahn train for Potsdam at around 7:15 AM, putting me in the city at 8 AM. I could enjoy some hot tea and breakfast at a café while the city was waking up, before getting started with sightseeing on the HOHO bus. Exactly as anticipated, my train pulled into the Potsdam metro station right on time. The Germans are known for their engineering prowess, so I expected nothing less—until I got off the train.

As I mentioned earlier, the Berlin metro system is vast, robust, and efficient. It is also largely wheelchair accessible, although some stations either only have an elevator on one side of the platform (who came up with *that* idea?) or no elevators at all. The city of Berlin offers several maps to indicate elevators' existence and location, and I had already checked to make sure that there were elevators at the station. However, in my haste and excitement, I forgot to check their operational status.

As soon as I exited the metro train, I saw a huge wooden enclosure around the space where the elevator was supposed to be. It was plastered with posters that indicated the elevator was under construction for an indefinite period of time. My stomach started sinking as the reality of my situation set in; to say I was crushed is the understatement of the century. I had absolutely no way to get down to the street level from the platform, and I felt my dreams of seeing Potsdam slowly fading away.

Not one to be easily deterred, I started conducting a search that I've done many times before — the feasibility of the next station over. Potsdam was at the very end of the S-bahn train line I was on, so I took a look at the elevator map of the previous station. *Yes! It had an elevator!* Better yet, it had a bus route that also went from that station to the city center of Potsdam. After waiting about 20 minutes for the next train heading in the direction from which I came, I boarded the metro once again, determined not to let the delay diminish my mood.

A mere five minutes later, I arrived at the neighboring Babelsberg metro station. I exited the train, rolled down to the end of the platform, and rounded the corner to take the elevator down to street level. At least, that was my plan until I saw that the elevator was broken. Not being repaired, not being renovated, just outright broken—like the direction in which my spirit was heading. I was running out of options, and quickly.

I only had one more station to the east from which I

could take a bus to the center of Potsdam. After waiting another 20 minutes, I hopped on the next train due east. Five minutes later, we pulled into the Griebnitzsee station. The doors opened, and I took a quick look at my surroundings. I didn't even exit the train. The neighborhood didn't look safe at all, let alone wheelchair friendly. I didn't think it would be a good idea to wait around for a bus by myself, so I resigned myself to my fate—I wouldn't see Potsdam after all. Then I promptly started to cry.

People who know me well know that I don't do tears. I understand that crying can be cathartic, and completely appropriate at certain times. However, for me, they generally don't accomplish anything. Tears don't solve any problems. While they can temporarily make me feel a little bit better, nothing truly makes me feel better than taking care of whatever started the tears in the first place. At that moment, I didn't know how to do that.

It's not often that I'm so brutally confronted with my disability. This isn't to say that I'm not reminded every single day of the fact I can't walk. It would be silly to think a wheelchair user can ignore this reality. While I live independently and manage very well in my wheelchair, I still understand that I have physical limitations. But somehow, I seem to have this incredible luck in that I'm always able to find a workaround or some alternate solution when faced with an obstacle to my movement. It seems, however, that my luck ran out in Berlin.

It didn't help that the previous day, I faced a similar problem. There are several small ferry boats that offer three-hour scenic tours on the Spree River through the heart of Berlin. I did my research and discovered that two of the tour company's vessels are wheelchair accessible. I figured out which of the multiple piers along the Spree River these boats used for docking and what times those two boats offered tours. They didn't provide reserved tour times, but I purchased my ticket and decided to show up early at the proper pier to make sure they had space for me.

It was about a 20-minute roll from my hotel to the pier, and it was a beautiful day for a three-hour river cruise. That is, until I realized that the only way from the sidewalk down to the boat dock was either by stairs or extremely steep dirt and grass hill. The boat was already at the dock, and a couple of crew members were preparing the boat for the cruise. I yelled down the stairs to explain my predicament, and they said that they could help me roll down the hill—which oddly is what they've done before. I felt really unsafe given the 45-degree incline of the hill, so I declined their offer with a considerable amount of disappointment, as well as disbelief that they would go through so much trouble to make a ferry boat accessible and not the dock. Welcome to the story of my life.

Now, here I was on a metro train headed back to Berlin, being faced with another major accessibility obstacle less than twenty-four hours later. I had a 45-minute train ride to do some thinking, and the whole situation reminded me about the competing theories of disability.

The primary theory of disability is the medical model. This basically says that we're disabled because we have something "wrong" with us. This could be a spinal cord injury, a chronic illness, a broken leg; you name it. Along with the medical model of disability comes the notion that people with disabilities somehow need to be "fixed" or cured, and that we would be much happier if we could walk again or if we weren't disabled at all. This presumes that healthy people who can walk are the norm, and we as a society should aspire to make everyone like that.

The alternate theory of disability is the social model. This theory posits that we are actually disabled by the world around us, rather than the physical state of our bodies. In essence, if there is a restaurant with a step to enter, I'm not disabled by the fact that I can't get up to walk and climb that step. I'm disabled by the step itself, and if that step were removed or overcome with a ramp, I would have the same physical ability to enter that restaurant as anyone else who can walk. The social model also aims to eliminate harmful assumptions that we are inherently suffering or unhappy simply because we're disabled, and promotes acceptance of people with disabilities as we are rather than people who need to be improved upon.

I had this disability model debate going on in my head that day on the Berlin train platform. When I first started using a wheelchair, I subscribed to the medical model. However, the more involved I became in the wheelchair community and disability rights movement, the more I understood the social model's value. The street level—my path to an amazing day in Potsdam—was being taken away from me by one of two things: my inability to walk down the steps to the street, or the broken elevator. It was my choice to make, and believe it or not, there are plenty of people with disabilities who go the route of the medical model. At that moment, it was tough for me to argue with the notion that I would've had a pretty fantastic day if that elevator had been working. So much for the miracle of German engineering.

It was roughly 11:30 AM by the time I got back into the city center, so a lunch of local currywurst and a nice cold Coke was going to hit the spot. I planned a very different day during my meal, but hopefully one that would bring joy, nonetheless. I was miraculously able to keep a previously canceled reservation to visit the dome on top of the Reichstag (the German Parliament). The original Reichstag building was designed beginning in 1894, and originally featured a very large dome. In 1933, the dome was destroyed in a fire thought to be set by communists (though no one knows for sure). The rest of the building suffered during the bombings of Berlin during World War II, and the eventual fall of Berlin to the Soviets in 1945. After the fall of communism, it was decided that the original Reichstag building should be rebuilt, along with a glass dome that emphasized a unified Germany.

As a wheelchair user, what I found fascinating about this colossal glass dome is that it offers a 360-degree view of Berlin via a huge spiral walkway all the way to the top. It's a double helix design, so you use a completely different ramp to work your way back down. The dome's center is a big funnel lined with mirrors that reflect the maximum amount of sunlight into the parliamentary chamber directly below. You can actually see into the chamber through the dome's glass floor, which serves as the center of the chamber's ceiling. The dome symbolizes the people being above the government, contrary to the situation under the Nazis.

The rest of my afternoon went swimmingly. I was on the

fence about visiting the German history museum only two blocks away from my hotel, but since I had nothing better to do, I decided to stop in. I was so glad I did because it turned out to be an absolutely fantastic experience. There was also a weekend arts and crafts fair going on right next door, and as I was rolling past the stalls, I heard a conversation between one of the vendors and some visitors about South Florida (where I grew up). It turned out that the artist and I went to high school together, and were only two grades apart with several mutual friends. Go figure!

Would I have had a better day in Potsdam had German engineering been on the ball that week? It's hard to say. Maybe I would have run into more obstacles with no alternate solutions somewhere in the city. Maybe it would've been fantastic. Of course, if I ever go back to Berlin, I now know to check the elevator outage map before attempting anything spontaneous. I also know at least I can try to see Potsdam again if I do make it out that way, so not all is lost if the elevators aren't working.

A few weeks earlier, I had posted something on my blog's Facebook page about my anxiety over visiting a place that would probably have a few obstacles to accessibility. One of my readers who frequently posts commented along the lines of my ability to make something good out of any bad situation. Usually, I can, but Berlin *really* tested my limits. *Remember the tears?* Maybe the day could have worked out better, but it still worked out pretty well. I'll take that over a day spent in bed or at home any day of the week.

9 FLYING THE UNFRIENDLY SKIES

Whether you're a wheelchair user or a marathon runner, I truly believe that most people who have ever flown on an airplane have a horror story.

If you're not a wheelchair user, most likely your horror story involves lost or destroyed luggage, extensive flight delays, flight cancellations, or sleeping on the ground at an airport. For wheelchair users, flying is our biggest fear and biggest nightmare. It can be hard to explain this point of view to people who can walk, but I'll give it a try.

Imagine that you've just boarded a flight with your spouse or significant other or best friend or paid escort for a dream vacation in Hawaii. You're staying at a gorgeous hotel on Waikiki Beach, you have reservations for a luau, and you've booked a tour to Diamondhead crater. For months, you've pictured drinking mai tais on a black sand beach and laughing through your first time on a surfboard during lessons. You've dropped a decent amount of money on a new vacation wardrobe, including those designer flip-flops that you'll probably never wear again.

After several hours in the air, your plane finally lands with a thud, and you're jolted awake from your reverie of Hawaiian sunsets. You and your travel partner exchange excited glances and squeals, and you start gathering your carry-on belongings. You patiently wait your turn to exit your row and start making your way down the aisle toward the door of the plane. You're about to step off the plane onto the jet bridge when, out of nowhere, a baggage handler whacks you so hard with a two-by-four that he breaks both of your legs. You immediately crumble to the floor in excruciating pain, completely unable to move, let alone walk.

You don't know whether to be angry at the baggage handler, angry at the airline which employs him, or simply petrified because you can't move. In the meantime, while you're screaming and crying, all the other passengers continue to get off the plane, awkwardly making their way around you (and your broken legs). Many of them steal a few glances at your situation, silently feeling sorry for your plight, but happy they can go on their way to their own Hawaiian dream vacations. Some offer to help, and others get angry because you're holding everything up. Your anxiety starts to skyrocket because, no matter the intention behind the attention, *everyone is focused on YOU.*

As for you, you have no idea what to do. Of course, a hospital trip is in order, but after that, what are your options? How can you enjoy your vacation with crutches, or worse, a manual wheelchair you have no familiarity with? Do you shed some tears, call it a day, and go home? Forget about that sunset horseback ride or those surfing lessons. At this point, you don't even know how you're going to take a shower, or even sit down on the toilet.

Welcome to the life of a wheelchair user who has to fly. This is the situation we are faced with every single time we get on an airplane. But, instead of our physical legs being broken, it's our figurative legs being broken—our wheelchairs. Since December 2018, when the Department of Transportation was forced to keep track of wheelchairs being lost or damaged by airlines, we learned that this is happening twenty-five times every day. Imagine the legs of twenty-five passengers being broken at the end of a flight every single day. Of course, that would result in billions of dollars' worth of lawsuits, airline stock prices tumbling, and scandals all across the news. But because it's our wheelchairs being broken and not actual legs, nobody really cares. Or, at least, that's what it feels like.

I needed to provide you with that context so I can tell

you the following three flying stories. I'll spoil it for you now and tell you that they all have a happy ending, but the conclusion isn't the lesson. Just bear with me.

By September 2017, I had traveled for about a year and a half with my electric scooter, and by some miracle had avoided any major damage. Sure, I had some scratches and some small pieces of chipped plastic here and there, but it was all cosmetic. However, after reading so many horror stories from fellow wheelchair users, I knew it was only a matter of time before the other shoe dropped and something happened to me—or more specifically, my figurative legs.

A few months earlier, I had found an accessible tour operator in Slovenia (formerly part of Yugoslavia in Central Europe). Wanting to visit almost anywhere in the world that had accessible tour opportunities, I jumped on their four-day city break package in and around the capital of Ljubljana. It didn't make any sense to fly all the way to Europe for just a four-day stay, so I planned an additional three-day holiday in my layover city of Frankfurt, Germany.

Frankfurt was fantastic, and the day came when I had to take the short flight from Frankfurt to Ljubljana. Everything was going fine at the Frankfurt airport, and as part of the boarding process, I was on my scooter in the Ambu-lift on the tarmac. An Ambu-lift is basically a truck where the compartment raises up on a scissor lift to allow the wheelchair user to roll onto the plane at the door level. Before raising up, I was transferred from my scooter to an aisle chair, where I would be strapped in and then rolled onto the plane to my seat. The ground crew then took my scooter to roll it the thirty or so yards to the cargo hold at the plane's back end. I was able to watch all of this from the Ambu-lift window.

I noticed something was wrong when they lifted my scooter onto the conveyor belt leading to the cargo hold. From my distant vantage point, I could tell that somehow the tire on the front wheel of my scooter had become dislodged from the rim. I have no idea how this happened, but can only speculate that the ramp crew forgot to put my scooter in neutral and somehow just dragged it the whole way to the back end of the plane. What I knew for sure was that I had a scooter on my plane that was unusable, and there was nothing I could do about it for the next hour.

By now, some of you may be thinking that I'm crazy or stupid for traveling by myself. I know it's a risk, and one that I willingly take every time I travel. If I had to wait around for someone to have the time or the money to travel with me as much as I do, I would be waiting for a really long time. Usually, the only solution for a situation like this would be to somehow manage in a manual chair long enough to get on a flight back home. Anyway, I would have to wait until we landed to see what was what.

Fortunately, my tour guide was waiting for me at the airport. The airport staff put me in a manual wheelchair and brought me to my guide in the arrivals hall. I met up with the ground crew, who brought me the scooter and showed me the problem. Indeed, the tire had come off the rim. They were worried about getting the rim back inside the tire because the rim was made of plastic, not metal. They were scared to crack it. I told them to do whatever they had to do, like they were doing surgery on a potentially fatal gunshot wound (*JUST SAVE IT!!!*), and to please be careful.

After half an hour of my tour guide valiantly trying to calm me down and keep me relaxed, the ground maintenance crew brought me my scooter in one piece. I had never felt such a sense of relief in my entire life! The scooter worked just fine for the rest of the trip, and for many trips afterwards. I will be eternally grateful for that ground crew in that little airport in the beautiful Slovenian city of Ljubljana.

Nightmare number two happened in April 2018 on my return flight from Lisbon, Portugal to Miami. I was already annoyed when I landed in Miami because I had paid extra for a bulkhead (first row) seat in the plane's center section. This allows me to have some extra legroom, and people don't have to shove me around while climbing over me to get to the lavatory. Apparently, TAP Portugal thought it was in my best interest to move me back twenty rows and place me in a designated wheelchair row, simply because the armrest lifts up. They did not reimburse me for the fee I paid for the bulkhead seat I lost. They also didn't tell me about the change before boarding. But at this point, that's neither here nor there.

The flight was uneventful, and we landed without incident at Miami International Airport. I'm always the last one off the plane because people have to come on the plane to roll me out. So, I waited patiently for everybody to disembark and for my wheelchair to be brought to the plane's door. There's this little law called the Air Carrier Access Act (ACAA) that requires any airline, whether domestic or foreign, that either arrives in or departs from the United States to comply with its tenets. One of those rules states that the airline has to return my wheelchair to the plane's door, or as close as possible on the jet bridge, within a reasonable amount of time—usually thirty minutes or less.

Well, thirty minutes came and went, and still no wheelchair. The airport crew was ready with the aisle chair to take me off the plane, but I told them that I would stay seated quietly (and comfortably) on the plane until my wheelchair was brought to me. We hit the 45-minute mark, and still no wheelchair. At that point, the airport representative for TAP Portugal got on the plane and approached me in a huff. I mean, he was *pissed*.

Every minute that I spent sitting on the plane was costing them money because they couldn't turn the plane around and get it moving for the next flight. However, I learned my lesson the hard way years before. If I got off the plane and sat in either a hard and uncomfortable aisle chair or in an airport manual wheelchair to wait for my personal chair to be brought to me, there would be no motivation for the airline to comply with the ACAA. So, I sat. And I waited some more. And the TAP guy started turning a shade of red-hot chili pepper.

In my years of flying as a wheelchair user, I have used dozens of airlines and flown over half a million miles. During that time, I have *never* had an airline representative yell at me. There's a first time for everything, and that was the day. He told me I was being ridiculous. He accused me of holding their plane hostage. He then told me he would call the police to have me forcibly removed from the plane. I unlocked my cell phone and went to hand it to him. He refused.

When situations like this happen to wheelchair users,

we're supposed to ask to speak to someone called a Complaint Resolution Official (CRO). Every airport is supposed to have at least one on duty during any time that flights are operating. This was not the case that day at MIA (another ACAA violation), so instead of the CRO they sent me someone else. He was nice. He was also very calm and very understanding.

He explained that because of the gate layout, the ground crew was physically unable to carry my scooter up the stairs to the jet bridge. He said they had initially sent it to the Customs area for collection, which is another common ACAA violation. Still, they would be able to roll it from Customs halfway down the jet bridge to a lounge area. If I were willing to get off the plane onto a manual chair, they would take me to that lounge area to be reunited with my scooter within 15-20 minutes. I shrugged my shoulders and said, "Okay."

Now, I may be crazy, but I'm not stupid. If the ramp agents were able to roll my scooter all the way from Customs halfway down the jet bridge to a lounge area, why couldn't they roll it just a few more down yards down the rest of the jet bridge to the door of the plane? This was still a violation of my rights as a disabled passenger. But at that point, I was ready to let it go. The stand-in CRO did his job in defusing the situation. He was kind, he was sympathetic, and he made me feel heard. He knew the situation was messed up, and while the solution wasn't ideal, it was clear that he was making a sincere effort to help me.

I later filed a complaint with both TAP Portugal and the Department of Transportation (DOT) for several ACAA violations. After *a full year*, I finally got a letter from the DOT with their investigation results. Basically, TAP denied any wrongdoing, but the DOT found them guilty of *all* the wrongdoing. I was never compensated in any way, and TAP was never punished in any way. But, at the end of the day, I made it home safely—with my scooter. I also learned to never fly with TAP again.

Nightmare number three happened at the end of one of the longest travel days of my life. No matter how you cut it, flying from the United States to mainland China is no easy task. In April 2019, I flew from Los Angeles to Shanghai on a direct Delta flight. The departure was delayed by six hours, so tack that on to a 14-hour flight, and my body was destroyed by the time we landed at midnight local time. However, I was excited to be in Shanghai in one piece and looking forward to my tour the next day. As always, I was the last one left on the plane, and waited patiently for my power chair to be brought to the door.

Thirty minutes passed, and nothing. I was starting to get concerned because Delta has a tracking system that allows me to find my chair's whereabouts—specifically, the last time that the attached Delta tag was scanned. Unfortunately, it appeared that the ground crew in Los Angeles forgot to scan the tag on my chair, so I had no way of knowing if my chair had even made it on the plane to Shanghai. China is also a tricky place because the government doesn't allow the plane crew to get off the plane onto the tarmac and help the local ground crew look for it.

I couldn't believe it, but the entire flight crew—pilots and all the flight attendants—waited on that empty plane with me while the Chinese ground crew looked for my power chair. Some of us chatted about my work and all the places I've been. The pilots were trying to communicate with employees at the airport. They even called Delta headquarters back in Atlanta to try to get some help. At the one-hour point, I was starting to panic. Shanghai isn't the most wheelchair accessible place in the world. While my ride from the airport to my hotel was waiting for me and knew I was delayed, it wouldn't be so easy to just get on a plane and turn around to go back to Los Angeles.

Finally, after seventy-five minutes, the pilot returned to our little group on the plane and happily announced that the ground crew had found my power chair in the Customs area. They even texted him a photo of the chair to confirm it was mine. All of us erupted in cheers, and I even cried a few tears of relief. I started profusely thanking each and every one of them for staying with me throughout the whole ordeal, especially after a 14-hour flight when I knew they were probably desperate to get off that plane and into a comfortable bed.

These are just the worst of my airline horror stories, and I have a few more here and there that are considerably less dramatic. I'm fortunate that I escaped from each one of them relatively unscathed. However, that certainly has not been the luck of many wheelchair users who have had their $30,000+ custom power chairs completely destroyed by various airline baggage handlers.

I hope that by reading this, other airline passengers will see us and be more patient and understanding about this deliberate process we must endure. But the common thread here is that people who care can make all the difference. The Ljubljana ground crew cared, the MIA airport stand-in CRO cared, and the Delta flight crew cared. In a world filled with shitty people—like a certain airline representative in Miami—and a travel lifestyle filled with delays and inconvenience, a smile and a kind word can really do wonders to turn a wheelie's bad day around.

10 HOW TO CARRY A TUNE

If there's anything I can't resist on a cruise, it's the fresh-baked cookies, the daily trivia contests, and a ship-wide singing competition.

I didn't start singing anywhere in public until I was 19 years old. Based on feedback from my mother before that, I really wasn't terrific. Like, at all. I started playing the piano when I was seven, but I was never really motivated to add vocals. However, in my late teens, I became obsessed with Tori Amos. I started singing along to songs of hers I knew how to play, mainly because I just couldn't help myself. A few years later, I discovered karaoke, which pretty much created a singing monster. I got much better over the years, and even had the chance to sing the National Anthem at a few military and professional sports events. Becoming a professional singer or musician has never been my dream, but winning a few karaoke competitions along the way has definitely given me some confidence in my skills.

As a wheelchair user, singing—or, more specifically, my continued ability to sing—has taken on a new significance. Because of my progressing MS, I have lost the dexterity in my hands required to play piano keys, and my feet can no longer move to use the foot pedals. One of the saddest days of my life was when I was forced to sell my baby grand piano after she spent sixteen years giving me pure joy. Singing is more challenging now from a seated position, but it's one of the physical things from my life before MS that I can still do. That gives it an extraordinary significance in my life.

As of April 2021, I have been on twenty-one cruises, sixteen of those as a wheelchair user, and almost every single one of those cruises had at least one karaoke night. One notable exception was a Holland America cruise where the average passenger's age was around 80 years old (although they did have a phenomenal string quartet). Needless to say, anyone who knows me knows where to find me on a cruise ship's karaoke night.

In May 2016, my best friend and I were aboard Princess Cruise Lines' *Star Princess* in Alaska when we learned that Princess was taking cruise karaoke to an entirely different level. The company had partnered with *The Voice*, the famous international TV singing competition, to select around a dozen of the ship's best singers during every cruise of seven nights or longer. They would then compete for the title of "Voice of the Ocean" on the main theater stage. The selection process was pretty simple. You would sing during one of the two karaoke nights, and members of the audience would then vote for the singers. The top ten passengers who got the most votes would compete in the final on the last night of the cruise.

I'm not gonna lie; the entire setup for the final show was extremely impressive. They had a massive digital screen wall as the stage backdrop, and even the three trademark high-back revolving chairs at stage right. The judges were two members of the ship's crew and the comic performer for that cruise. My best friend Erin is an incredible singer, and both of us made the final. However, we all had to figure out how to get me and my electric scooter onto the main stage. This was the first-ever "Voice of the Ocean" competition for Princess, so it was a learning experience for everyone involved. As someone who is very breakable thanks to wheelchair-induced osteoporosis, the prospect of getting carried through tight quarters by strangers with no caregiving experience made me *really* nervous. The thought of them dropping (and potentially damaging) my scooter just added another layer of anxiety.

Fortunately, the ship was built in such a way that I could roll in my scooter through the hidden crew corridors and use the crew elevators to reach the lower level of the backstage area. I don't weigh very much and neither did my scooter, so the crew just decided it would be easiest to carry both of us up the seven or so stairs to the main stage level for rehearsal and the live performance. It's a good thing that was an option because I ended up winning the competition. Three years later, I won my second "Voice of the Ocean" trophy on the *Crown Princess* in the Caribbean. That time, instead of carrying me up the stairs, the inventive crew constructed a wooden wheelchair ramp from scratch. I'm still mentally recovering from getting pushed up and eased down that makeshift ramp at a 45-degree angle, but I appreciated the effort.

So, when I sang during karaoke night on the *Island Princess* in February 2019 to compete for my third trophy, I thought nothing of it. As expected, I made the top ten, so I started practicing my chosen song for the competition's first rehearsal with the live band two days later. The afternoon after I found out I was a finalist, I got a phone call in my stateroom. It was the ship's cruise director, and in a weighty and regretful tone, he informed me that there was no way to get me onto the stage safely, and as a result, I would not be able to compete in the final show.

At first, I laughed it off. I told him not to worry, I had done this twice before on other Princess ships, and they could simply carry me up onto the stage. He then explained that because the *Island Princess* was an older ship, the stage area and the surrounding corridors were not built the same way as those on the *Star* or *Crown*. Specifically, there was no accessible path from the passenger area to the crew corridor to access an elevator to reach the backstage area. It also didn't make sense from a production perspective to try to carry me and my small power wheelchair onto the stage from the theater floor. My stomach dropped.

I was crushed, but not for the reason you might think. I had already won two of these competitions on other Princess ships, so it definitely wasn't about winning. It was all about the ability—or in this case, my lack of ability—to participate in a fun and exciting activity just like everyone else. I was also really pissed off that they didn't tell me before I sang in the karaoke preliminary that I wouldn't be able to compete in the final. And I wasn't the only person using mobility aid; there was a scooter user who sang in the preliminary, and although he didn't make the top ten, the cruise director's staff didn't give him a heads up about the logistical situation, either. Finally, I was angry that they approached me with only the problem without even thinking that there might be a solution. I felt like my right to equal access wasn't worth considering.

After the brief phone call ended, I did what I usually do when I need to vent about a situation where I'm excluded from something because of my wheelchair—I took to Facebook, without expecting anything to come of it. I explained the entire situation in detail, and made sure to tag Princess Cruise Lines so they would hopefully see it. Within a couple of hours, over two hundred and sixty of my travel blog's social media followers had commented on or shared the post, and Princess was getting pinged with every share. One of my sorority sisters, an experienced travel agent, made a phone call to a vice president she knew at Princess to explain my situation—which she made clear needed to be corrected immediately.

Let's just say that Princess Cruise Lines clearly got the message. The following morning, I had a brief meeting with Cruise Director, who said the crew had brainstormed and come up with a "unique" solution to get me onto the stage. It would take some creativity on their part and a lot of flexibility on my part, but I was definitely up for the challenge. Here's how things went down on the final evening of the cruise.

For whatever reason, the Cruise Director's staff had decided to schedule the final rehearsal to end roughly one hour before the final show would begin. This actually would work out quite well for me because I would only have to get maneuvered onto and off the stage once. On the day of the show, all the performers had to meet in the theater at noon for a rundown of how the show would proceed. While they climbed up the steps to the stage to prepare for the rehearsal, I was told to rendezvous with the crew members at a designated point on one of the outdoor walkways. My adventure was about to begin.

I was quickly met by a handsome Italian officer in charge of the ship's food and beverage department in his crisp white uniform, along with four young European crew members. Those four men were carrying what looked like a combination between a cheap sling beach chair and a moving dolly. It turned out that contraption was an emergency evacuation chair, and it's what they were going to use to get me onto the stage. I also learned that the crew was excited to carry me in it because they rarely had a chance to practice evacuation drills with an actual disabled passenger. *Uh-huh. Meet Sylvia, the singing guinea pig.*

They didn't give me any time to have second thoughts because we had to get a move on. First, I had to transfer from my comfortable power wheelchair into this...*thing*, which was an awkward transition at best. It's constructed so that the passenger manages to stay in an upright position no matter how the four crew members are holding each corner handle of the chair. It wasn't long before I realized how necessary this feature was going to be.

After picking me up, we headed toward a bulkhead door with a red sign that said CREW ONLY. The Italian officer opened the door, we all entered the cramped crew area, and in front of me was what appeared to be a sheer drop to the deck below. As we moved closer to the edge, I quickly realized there was a ridiculously minimal metal ladder that was desperately attempting to impersonate some semblance of steps. "We're going to go down that thing???" I managed to squeak out to one of my litter carriers. He smiled brightly at me and replied, "Oh, yes," with a thick Slavic accent. "You be OK, no worry!" There was that smile again. I'm pretty sure he would have given me two thumbs up if he had any free hands.

Fortunately, the trip down that ladder was slow, methodical, and completely uneventful. We traveled through a maze of corridors, then finally reached the backstage area. They couldn't physically carry me up and down the stairs between the green room and the stage for liability reasons. Instead, they had a manual wheelchair set up for me just offstage to use during the rehearsal and the show. So, my entourage continued up those stairs, and I safely transferred from the emergency sling to the manual wheelchair, where I would remain until the end of the show.

To be clear, this was not an ideal situation. I knew I would not have access to a bathroom during the roughly three hours I would be in the theater, so I made sure not to eat or drink anything beforehand and use the bathroom right before I met with the crew. I fit somewhat awkwardly in the one-size-fits-all manual wheelchair, and maneuvering it successfully would take some practice since I'm not really used to them as a power chair user. I also wouldn't have access to all the snacks and goodies in the green room with my fellow performers.

All this being said, my fellow passengers and the crew were absolutely amazing. The other singers and crewmembers offer to bring me any snacks I wanted from the green room, and came just to hang out with me so I wouldn't feel alone backstage. I was able to use as much time as I needed to get comfortable with the manual wheelchair and figure out the timing to roll onto my mark on the stage for the live show—which I won, by the way.

No, that's not meant to be a spoiler, and no, I'm not going to go into the details of the actual show. That's not what this story is about. For my disabled readers, it's about fighting for the equal access you want and deserve. In some cases, the fight can get ugly, and I was prepared to go there the second I hit the post button on that Facebook status update. Fortunately, I was sailing with a company that valued me as a passenger and a paying customer and realized it was in their best interest to help make things work. I give credit where credit is due, and I was more than happy to post a subsequent Facebook update giving my thanks to all the crew members and staff who made that experience possible.

For my non-disabled readers, I hope this story helps you understand that where there's a will, there actually is a way. That's not just a tired cliché. It sucks that wheelchair users have to rely on society at large to have the will to make equal access a reality for us. There really is only so much we can do. However, sometimes the best thing we can do is have a conversation, be flexible, and be creative. If I hadn't taken action after that phone call, I would have left that ship with a lot of disappointment and at least a small amount of bitterness. Granted, the initial motivation for Princess to get their shit together was the potential for bad press, and had I initiated the conversation on the ship to push for a fix, things may have been resolved more quickly. But, once they decided to put their heads together, they came up with a solution that worked for everybody. Hopefully, that will make a difference in future competitions on that ship when a wheelchair user wants to sing.

I know not every wheelchair user will have the same sense of adventure, or even the physical ability to safely use that evacuation and manual chair combination—or any other alternative method of getting from point A to point B. The point is to at least have the conversation and exhaust every possible option before giving up. We do this almost every single day of our lives as wheelchair users and people with disabilities. When the corporate world, the travel sector, and society at large decide they're willing to meet us halfway, there's no limit to what we can do.

We be okay; no worry.

11 THE SOUND OF GRAY

It was raining on the day I visited the Auschwitz-Birkenau concentration and extermination camps in Poland.

The small drops were falling lightly on the sidewalk outside my hotel that morning with a relaxing whisper. The weather was completely appropriate to set the mood for what was arguably going to be one of the most challenging days of my traveling life. I don't know about you, but I think it would be strange to visit a place where millions of Jews were tortured and executed on a sunny and cloudless day. I didn't want to be happy on this day. I wanted to be sad. And wet. And cold. And uncomfortable. As they say, be careful what you wish for.

I had the opportunity to visit Auschwitz-Birkenau during a trip to Poland in 2017 after discovering a local accessible tour operator. I spent part of that time in Warsaw and the other part in Kraków, my departure point for this day trip. For many years before this visit, I had been fascinated by aspects of World War II. Many years earlier, while I was on active duty in the Air Force (and still walking), I made pilgrimages to Normandy and the infamous D-Day beaches, as well as the sunken USS Arizona Memorial in Hawaii's Pearl Harbor. I learned a lot about the sacrifices that American and Allied soldiers made in fighting against the Germans and the Japanese. I tried to imagine what it must have been like to drag myself out of those English Channel waters, knowing I had at least a 10 percent chance of getting killed before I reached the sand. Fundamentally, my World War II education was based on a purely American point of view.

I knew the basics of Polish history during that time, but only on paper. I knew they were one of the first countries occupied by the Nazis, only to turn around after emerging from the war and become occupied by the Soviets. I knew of, and more importantly, really believed in, the Holocaust, during which the Nazis exterminated over six million Jews. The majority of them were killed in Poland. Outside of that, I was quite ignorant of my latest destination, and truly had no idea what to expect.

My first stop was in Warsaw for a few days, and it didn't take me long to fall in love with the city. It's large by any European standard, and very modern, with shiny skyscrapers, clean public transportation, and beautiful parks. It was also surprisingly easy for me to roll around by myself in my wheelchair, with just a few obstacles here and there. I was classically trained on piano starting at the age of seven, so I was quite embarrassed to realize I didn't know that Chopin was Polish and originally from Warsaw. It was amazing to see churches where he played as a young prodigy, and the exterior of the church where his heart is nestled inside of a pillar.

In Warsaw, there were plenty of visual reminders of the Soviet occupation, especially with some older buildings. When I went to the "old town" section of the city, essentially the historic city center, I was expecting to see more clear evidence of the Nazi occupation and destruction. However, everything looked so beautiful, clean, and well-maintained. The buildings were colorful, historically accurate, and looked freshly painted—even the old (or so I thought) Royal Castle.

After learning that the Royal Castle was wheelchair accessible, I rolled inside to take a tour. In the entry foyer, that was the first time I got a real glimpse into the Polish experience with the Nazis. According to the then-and-now aerial photographs, the beautiful castle I was sitting in, surrounded by beautiful tapestries, furniture, chandeliers, and paintings, was nothing but rubble a few decades earlier. Around 95 percent of central Warsaw was nothing but ash and dust after the Nazis were done with it.

Initially built in the 14th century, the Nazis had embedded dynamite in the castle walls and mostly destroyed it in 1944. Thanks to donations from the United States, combined with architectural and design drawings that survived, the castle was completely rebuilt in the 1970s. After my tour, I went back outside took a look around at the entirety of Warsaw's Old Town. Although everything looked historic, most of what I was seeing was only a few decades old. I remembered standing on Omaha Beach in Normandy in 2002 and looking out across the English Channel, trying to picture hundreds of naval vessels with thousands upon thousands of soldiers storming the beach. Now I tried to imagine my current surroundings in black and white, amid a post-apocalyptic scene with nothing but ash raining down from the sky. It was surreal, to say the least.

After no small amount of frustration at the Warsaw train station the next day, I hopped on a short two-hour train ride from Warsaw to Kraków. To say I fell in love with Kraków is an understatement. It has an entirely different look and feel than Warsaw, probably because much of it is historical with a medieval vibe, with not as many modern areas as Warsaw. It sits on the Vistula River and goes back to the 7th century, so I certainly had a lot of scenery and history to fill my culture tank. I spent hours in the main square, eating, people watching, fighting with the cobblestones, and just gazing at my surroundings.

Physically, Kraków fared much better than Warsaw with regards to destruction by the Nazis. However, it became the Nazi General Government's capital, and the most significant source of deportees to the Auschwitz concentration camp. More than 200,000 Jews were rounded up and forced to live in the Kraków ghetto, which I was able to explore with a guide. Some of those were selected by Oskar Schindler to work in his enamelware factory (members of Schindler's list), effectively saving them from execution by the Nazis (more on this later). My guide told me fascinating stories of some more well-known Jews who lived in the ghetto before their deportation, as well as some who went to extraordinary lengths to escape.

I woke up on the morning of my day trip to Auschwitz-Birkenau and saw that it was cold and raining. The weather, combined with all the information I had learned in the previous days in the Kraków ghetto and the Warsaw Royal Castle, put me in a mood that I felt had prepared me somewhat for what I was about to experience.

I could not have been more wrong.

Auschwitz-Birkenau is a massive complex of camps and buildings. The Auschwitz portion was the labor camp, and the Birkenau portion was the extermination camp. My guide dropped me off in our accessible van at the Auschwitz visitors' center. You're not allowed to walk around Auschwitz on your own. You must be part of a tour, which departs the visitors center roughly every fifteen minutes. I was assigned to an English-speaking tour guide and given a headset with a receiver to hear her narration. You are also strongly advised to remain quiet and respectful, and thankfully, all my fellow visitors followed this advice. However, that silence felt unnatural in such a large outdoor space, and often weighed so heavily that it became deafening in the gray air.

My driver was initially going to allow me to go on the tour on my own, but after attempting to roll in my three-wheeled scooter for just a few dozen yards, he realized he would need to keep me company and help me out of a few jams. The ground of the Auschwitz camp is unpaved. It's original, consisting of leftover crumbling and crushed brick, stone, pebbles, and rocks. There's also a lot of sand and gravel. Mix that with a steady rain that started overnight, and you've got a nasty, mushy, muddy mix that was extremely difficult to maneuver on three small wheels. I got stuck and had to get pulled out of potholes many times.

I knew I wouldn't be able to go inside any of the buildings. Fortunately, with my headset, I heard a fair amount of what the tour guide was saying inside each block to the rest of my group. There were also large informational signs in English outside the more significant buildings. It didn't take long before I was actually grateful that I couldn't go inside and see the things the guide was discussing.

Everybody reacts to information about things that are seemingly impossible in different ways. Some people laugh, some people express outright disbelief, and others simply go silent. During the first hour of my visit, I made a point to observe the people around me and how they were reacting. I had no idea who my fellow tourists were. Were they curious foreigners? Were they Holocaust survivors or family members? Jewish, Muslim, or Christian? Pretty much everyone was silent and respectful. I was doing okay…until the hair. That was the point at which I started to go numb.

Some people are more meticulous about their hair than others, but generally speaking, it's not something that humans are overly concerned with – let's say, compared to paying the bills or feeding our kids. Oddly enough, we typically don't place a ton of value on our hair…until we lose it. I'm not talking about a bad haircut. Psychologically speaking, it can be devastating for some men to start going bald, and for many women to lose their hair to chemotherapy, alopecia, or other medical conditions. Hair often represents masculinity for men and femininity for women. Now, imagine losing your hair to the Nazi industrial complex.

Prisoners at all Nazi concentration camps had all of their body hair removed upon arrival. This was to prevent typhus, which spread by body lice. It was also removed from corpses taken out of the gas chambers. However, all of this hair was not thrown away. According to a 1993 article in *The New Yorker* by Timothy Rybek, "German felt and textile manufacturers used the versatile fibre in the production of thread, rope, cloth, carpets, mattress stuffing, lining stiffeners for uniforms, socks for submarine crews, and felt insulators for the boots of railroad workers." Human hair "was often used in delayed action bombs, where its particular qualities made it highly useful for detonating purposes." Just imagine if strands of your hair were used to make a bomb that would later kill dozens of your friends and family members.

Then…there are the shoes. Piles and piles of shoes are some of the most common displays around the world used to remember the Holocaust. This is because thousands of shoes were removed from corpses every day during the peak of the Nazi gassing of Jews at concentration camps. There are currently 110,000 shoes at Auschwitz—many of them formerly belonging to children.

However, the collection that hit hardest for me was an

enormous pile of prosthetic limbs and crutches that were brought into the camp by Polish war veterans of World War I. According to the United Kingdom's Holocaust Memorial Day Trust, severely mentally and physically disabled people and those perceived to have disabilities were targeted because of Nazi beliefs that they were a burden to both society and the state. Between 1933 and 1939, the Nazis forcibly sterilized 360,000 people thought to be mentally ill. Years later, I saw some of these artifacts in person at the Holocaust Memorial Museum in Washington, DC.

In 1939, the killing of disabled children and adults began. All children under the age of three who had illnesses or a disability, such as Down's syndrome or cerebral palsy, were targeted under a euthanasia program called T4. Following the outbreak of war in September 1939, the program was expanded. The Germans set up six killing centers, but the original execution methods—lethal injection and starvation—were considered too slow for larger numbers of people. That's when the experimental gassing began. Victims were sent to gas chambers disguised as shower rooms. The concept for these chambers was later exported to Auschwitz-Birkenau, and it's estimated that over 250,000 people with disabilities were murdered by the Nazis during this time.

At the time of learning this information, I had been at the camp for about two hours. I still had more to see, but the rest of my visit passed in a strange haze. The rain stopped and started, and my fingers were numb from the damp cold. My driver was very kind and held my umbrella as I struggled to maneuver my scooter through mud, over rocks and pebbles, and through potholes. I had a tough time absorbing and processing, so everything seemed to go through me. I stopped to take pictures, all of which I would edit later into high-contrast black and white or sepia-toned images. I determined that color had no place here.

Shortly afterward, we left Auschwitz and only made a very brief stop at the neighboring Birkenau extermination camp. This is where Jews were taken like cattle in railcars from Auschwitz to be gassed, and then burned. Much of it was destroyed by the Nazis during their retreat to eliminate as much evidence as possible, but parts of the original structures remain. Some of the wooden barracks are being restored, and the brick barracks that used to house women still stand. However, the Nazis dynamited four crematoria—something I was grateful for, so I wouldn't have to envision the plumes of black smoke, the smell of burned flesh, and the falling ash.

Even though I arrived back at my hotel in Kraków at the reasonable hour of 3 PM, I knew I had neither the physical nor emotional energy to move from my bed. *Schindler's List* came out in 1993, and twenty-four years later, I still hadn't seen it. Well...that was the day. I shed not one tear during my visit to Auschwitz-Birkenau, but they came out tenfold while I lay on the bed watching this gut-wrenching movie on my tablet in the dark. They filmed many scenes on location, and it was incredibly surreal to know that I had been there just a few hours earlier. I physically saw the remnants of those chimneys that were now spewing black smoke and ash on my screen, and it hit me like a sledgehammer to fully realize they weren't Hollywood set props. I asked myself, *How can human beings do this to each other and believe it's fully justified?* Even worse, I wondered how some people could believe this never happened at all.

The following day was sunny and cloudless. I rolled in my chair for almost half an hour through the city, including some sketchy industrial parts of Kraków, to reach Oskar Schindler's enamel factory. For some background, if you're one of the three people on the planet who haven't watched the Oscar-winning movie (like I was), Schindler was a member of the Nazi party and an agent of the Abwehr (German military intelligence). In late 1939, he took over the receivership of the factory, which produced pots and pans for field kitchens and ammunition shells — making it a critical part of the war effort.

In 1943, Schindler helped establish a sub-camp of the Plaszów concentration camp, where the prisoners who worked in his factory lived. Schindler's Abwehr connections helped him protect his Jewish workers from deportation and extermination. However, he had to pay the Germans a considerable amount in bribes to keep them from becoming too curious. During the factory's peak in 1944, it employed approximately 1,750 workers, about 1,000 of whom were Jews under Schindler's protection. He went bankrupt from paying bribes and buying supplies for his workers, and later lived on the support he received from the Jews he saved until he died in 1974. Only the factory façade is original, but the museum inside is still an intense experience.

Since I visited Auschwitz-Birkenau, I've been to at least half a dozen European countries where Jews were arrested and deported to concentration camps in Poland or Germany. If you walk or roll along the street in a city in one of these countries, you may look down and notice small brass squares embedded in the sidewalk. These are called *Stolperstein* in German, meaning "stumbling stone." Engraved on these small plaques are the names of the Jews who lived or worked in the buildings in front of these plaques, when they were born and their estimated year of death, and the concentration camp to which they were deported.

As of October 2018, over 70,000 *Stolpersteine* in 1,200 cities across more than a dozen countries had been laid, making the 1992 project by German artist Gunter Demnig the world's largest decentralized memorial. Many American visitors to Europe don't know what they are, but upon close inspection, they can probably hazard a good guess. I'm very proud every time I have the opportunity to teach someone their meaning, and equally crushed every time I see them.

They're harsh reminders that, had I been born in a different place at another time, my physical condition and supposedly resulting societal burden would have been deserving of extermination. I'm pretty sure that the majority of people today no longer feel that way about people with disabilities. However, I'm not so sure they don't still see us as a burden—on society, on the healthcare system, on our families. I also often think about other people in my life who the Nazis would have gladly murdered. While I know our circumstances and struggles are different, it's sobering to know that we share this common thread. Our battle is no longer surviving extermination by a tyrannical government, but we're still fighting for the hearts and minds of our neighbors.

12 THAT TIME I SAID THE 'C' WORD IN BELFAST

I never thought I'd be in a place where I had to look over my shoulder after casually name-dropping my religion of choice in public.

One of the unusual benefits of being a longtime U2 fan is that you learn more than you ever intended about Irish history and politics. However, the downside is that your newfound knowledge about the schism between Ireland and Northern Ireland might lead you to believe that Belfast is some bombed-out shell of a city more akin to 1990s Sarajevo than smiling Irish eyes. Fortunately, all it took was a highly addictive, critically acclaimed, and award-winning cable TV series to turn things around for this capital city. Sort of.

Before I visited Belfast in August 2018, I primarily associated Northern Ireland with "The Troubles." This was a three-decade conflict from roughly the late 1960s to the late 1990s between Irish Republicans (who were mostly Catholic) and Ulster Unionists (who were mostly Protestant), although the roots of this division go back to the 17th century. Contrary to popular American belief, Northern Ireland is not an independent country (or a region of Ireland proper), but rather a part of the United Kingdom. To drastically oversimplify, the Republicans wanted Northern Ireland to become part of a unified Ireland, and the

Unionists wanted it to remain part of the United Kingdom. I always thought it was a war between Catholics and Protestants, but there wasn't a religious aspect to it, per se. However, society dictated that your religion automatically assigned you to one political faction or the other. You'll need to remember this later.

If you've spent any time working in counterterrorism like I did for over twelve years, you've heard of the Irish Republican Army (IRA). Same if you've seen Harrison Ford play the role of Jack Ryan in *Patriot Games*. This, combined with the brutal lyrics of U2's 80s hit "Sunday Bloody Sunday," was the picture I had in my head of Belfast and Northern Ireland as a whole. That is, until I (and basically the whole world) was introduced to the cinematic landscape eye candy that is the HBO series *Game of Thrones*.

The show was filmed in many incredibly scenic locations worldwide, including Iceland, Spain, and Croatia. However, the main soundstage and the bulk of the series' production staff were located in Belfast, as are some of the most iconic scene sites. The show became so huge, and fans became so involved, that *Game of Thrones* tours started popping up in all of these countries— especially in Northern Ireland. Belfast is also the birthplace of the *Titanic*, so it was a no-brainer to build the fantastic *Titanic* museum right on the spot where the historic luxury ocean liner was launched—coincidentally, a stone's throw and phone camera zoom away from the *Game of Thrones* soundstage. Tourists started flocking to a revitalized Belfast, and it started looking like Northern Ireland could finally put its 'troubled' past behind it.

After doing my standard accessibility research, I was thrilled to discover that Belfast would not only be doable, but relatively easy, and so would other parts of Northern Ireland. Because it's part of the United Kingdom, Belfast has a ton of London black taxis. All of these have a built-in ramp, and although space inside can be a little cramped, it makes pretty much every London cab wheelchair accessible. Luckily for me, several of these taxi companies offered wheelchair accessible tours. The first one I picked? Take a wild guess.

In addition to filming locations like the Dark Hedges (the King's Road), Ballintoy Harbour (the Iron Islands), and Cushendun Caves (Melissandre's cave on Dragonstone), we visited Dunluce Castle (where I got carried *while still sitting on my scooter* up and down several steps), the glorious Giant's Causeway (where my scooter battery fought for dear life), and the Antrim Coast (where I tried on Cersei's actual crown at the official series jeweler). But as breathtaking as this full-day landscape-porn tour was, it wasn't anywhere near as intense as my two-hour city tour of Belfast the following day.

I'm having a hard time deciding how to explain the surreal nature of driving around Belfast shortly after learning what happened there as recently (relatively speaking) as my high school graduation. The look and layout of the city itself weren't anything out of the ordinary for me. I visited Dublin in April 2017, and a lot of things looked similar—residential areas with nondescript late 18th- and early 19th-century façades, cobblestones here and there, shops, restaurants, and of course, a pub on every corner. What I didn't know until my tour guide started narrating was that we were driving through one former war zone after another.

These neighborhoods were strictly divided between Catholic and Protestant, between Republican and Union loyalist. There were so many remaining signs of these divisions everywhere, including old fences and dozens of prominent flags everywhere announcing resident loyalties. During "The Troubles," the predominantly Protestant police cracked down hard on Catholics, which resulted in the rise of a resistance comprised of local militias and IRA terrorists. Neighbors kidnapped and bombed and assassinated each other. No police officer or loyalist politician felt safe, and with good reason. Gunfire in the streets of Belfast was an almost daily occurrence, as was the notorious calling card of the IRA, the car bomb. I know there are some pretty bad neighborhoods in many American cities, but I can't fathom living with that level of violence and chaos anywhere in the US like it's a typical daily occurrence.

Mind you, this was going on for *thirty years*. And if that wasn't crazy enough, it was virtually impossible to tell the Catholics and the Protestants apart just by looking at them. However, everyone knew where they lived, down to the street block. Catholics went to school with Catholics, and Protestants went to school with Protestants. Your son Johnny wants to play with Mary's son Bobby? You'd better find out where they go to church first because their daddies might be trying to kill each other after work.

Fortunately, negotiations between all parties finally began in 1993, a cease-fire was enacted in 1997, and The Good Friday power-sharing agreement was signed in 1998, formally ending "The Troubles." At least, on paper. The signs and symbols are still everywhere in the city, particularly in the famous mural art spread out all over Belfast. You can see these political statements manifested on concrete walls, on the sides of stores, and climbing six stories high on hotel or apartment building exteriors. The militias still have their headquarters buildings, and some are considered active. The IRA evolved into the Real IRA, then the New IRA, which is still conducting terrorist bombings in Northern Island and across the United Kingdom.

I'm explaining all of this history because it's essential context for my meeting with Rachel (which isn't her real name). There are plenty of bad things about social media, but one of the really great things is that it has allowed me to connect with so many people in the disability space that I would otherwise never get a chance to meet. I'm a member of a couple of Facebook groups for women who use wheelchairs, and that's how I "met" Rachel. I found her interesting right away because she's a musician – specifically, a guitarist – who uses a manual wheelchair, and a member of a popular local rock band. She also lives in Belfast, so we made arrangements to meet up during my visit at an accessible coffee shop close to my hotel.

Meeting up with friends who use wheelchairs in foreign countries is a vastly different experience than here in the United States. When I travel abroad, I always stay in the city center as close as possible to the bigger attractions, restaurants, shops, etc., because this tends to be the most wheelchair accessible part of any city. I know in my head that there are wheelchair users among the millions of people who live in residential neighborhoods across foreign cities. Still, until I met up with Rachel, I'd never had the opportunity to discuss in detail what that experience is like. Spoiler alert: it's not pretty.

Belfast is a modern city, but it's still part of Europe, which means that it's old—at least, by American standards. City centers in Europe are mostly wheelchair accessible because city planners have made them that way to attract tourists of all ages and abilities. They're not as motivated to improve accessibility for locals in the suburbs and residential areas because it's not bringing in the tourist dollars. Also, many European countries don't have an equivalent to the Americans with Disabilities Act, so citizens can't complain or sue anyone if they can't use the local bus or buy a pint at their favorite pub.

Rachel described to me with considerable dismay how inaccessible her current living situation was. Being a manual wheelchair user gave her a little flexibility because the big wheels allowed her to overcome some minor obstacles by popping a wheelie. However, she still had steps to her front door, and there were no real modifications for accessibility in her home. She lived with a boyfriend who could provide a lot of assistance, but truly independent living was not an option for her.

Rachel had also chosen a career path filled with physical obstacles. As a local rock band member, her gigs were almost always in smaller bars or venues — and often one or two floors up. She explained how she would have to get out of her wheelchair and literally drag herself up one or two flights of stairs while her bandmates would carry her wheelchair and guitar. If she was lucky, she might be able to maneuver her chair into something that could vaguely be described as a functioning toilet stall during breaks.

I was fascinated listening to Rachel telling me all about her daily life in a place that clearly wasn't designed for people like us. We must have chatted for hours about family, life as wheelchair users, music, and all sorts of other things. We talked for so long that the coffee shop closed down and we had to take our conversation outside. It was lightly drizzling, but we found a large awning to duck under so Rachel could smoke a cigarette while we spoke.

When I travel, I'm the type of person who wants to know anything and everything about a country, and even more so if I'm able to elicit that information from a local. I want to ask the hard and uncomfortable questions about politics, religion, immigration, race relations; you name it. Otherwise, the only places where I can learn about these things are international cable news stations or the Internet, and those aren't always the most reliable sources of information. To be fair, Rachel isn't an ambassador or the elected representative of everyone in Belfast. Still, I was pretty sure she had a better handle on the situation in Northern Ireland than anybody else I knew.

For some horrible reason I can't recall at the moment, I thought that would be a good time to start talking about my experience during my recent city tour of Belfast. Just to be clear, Rachel and I are outside on the sidewalk, in public, with plenty of cars and people passing by. Within earshot. And being Cuban, when I get worked up or excited about something, I get loud. Very loud. With lots of violent hand movements that draw attention and clearly identify me as a non-local. In my enthusiasm over explaining to Rachel how fascinating I found her hometown's history, I failed to notice her subtle body language indicating her increasing discomfort. Still, she was listening patiently, if a bit fidgety...until I uttered the 'C' word. More specifically, I loudly made reference to the fact I was Catholic.

Rachel's body language went from subtle to head-on-a-swivel in a hurry. I finally picked up on the signals she was sending when she started looking around to see if anyone had overheard the obnoxiously loud Cuban woman inadvertently broadcasting a loose affiliation with IRA terrorists. That was when *my* paranoia kicked in, and I started scanning the faces and movements of everyone within a 15-yard radius. *Is anyone watching us? Did anyone hear what I just said? Would anyone actually threaten us?* I was quickly reminded of how vulnerable we were as two women in wheelchairs capable of neither fight nor flight. I also very quickly changed the subject.

After a few uncomfortable minutes passed, our visit came to a natural conclusion as dinnertime approached. As I accompanied Rachel to her car, neither one of us acknowledged the strange hiccup in time that had just transpired. We hugged and said our goodbyes, and as I rolled back to my hotel, I wondered if she had noticed that I had noticed her trying to notice if anyone had noticed our conversation. "The Troubles" may have technically ended, but the worry still lingered.

During my train ride to Dublin the following day for my flight home, I had a lot about Belfast to mentally unpack. When we travel abroad and come across something, well…foreign, it's human nature to try to relate it to something we're familiar with. I think it's just something we do to make ourselves feel more comfortable in unfamiliar surroundings. For example, Vienna and Prague's historic city centers both remind me of Disney World in their architectural perfection, and the endless seas of grapevines outside of Cape Town remind me of my four years spent living near Napa Valley in California. I can even relate more serious issues like immigration problems and racism in foreign countries to the problems we experience in the United States.

But I had absolutely nothing to grab onto when it came to politics and the associated violence and religious connections in Northern Ireland. You'll soon read my chapter on my visit to Israel, and that's the closest I can come to a similarity—the subtle but unmistakable undercurrent that something bad could potentially happen at any time and in any place. Yet, all I could think of was that I didn't know most of my friends' religious preferences back home. Based on social media posts and personal relationships, I knew who most of my Jewish friends were, a couple of Muslim friends, and a couple of friends who practiced Buddhism. I also knew who some of my atheist friends were. But if you asked me to guess the division of my Christian friends between Catholic and Protestant? I would say I had no better than a 50-50 chance.

I'm no longer a practicing Catholic, but my two children are still being raised that way. I'm trying to imagine explaining to them that they wouldn't be allowed to play with the neighbor's kids because they go to a Baptist church. Dating and marriage might be different because I know that religious differences can be a nonstarter for some people. However, there's probably an excellent chance that your family members wouldn't attempt to bomb or assassinate or kidnap each other if you did try to cross those religious lines in the sack.

Then I think back to Rachel, and I wonder what it must

be like to live in a place like Belfast every day with that undercurrent running through your existence. I don't know if she even practices religion because it didn't matter to me, so I didn't ask. I don't know what her politics are for the same reason. Maybe she's grown numb or immune to the whole thing because that's just what her everyday life is like, and she was born towards the very end of that time period.

As a fellow wheelchair user, I couldn't help myself from asking even more complex questions. If Rachel was out in public and fell out of her chair or ran into trouble in some way, would someone rush to help her if they somehow magically knew their religious preferences didn't align? Did her bandmates care about each other's religions? Did their fans? Now, this is something I can definitely relate to current events in the United States. Don't some Americans already avoid dating each other or letting their kids play together or maybe even helping each other based on racial or political differences? Our history in the last century is nowhere near as extreme, but we're not strangers to racial and political violence. While I have no idea if this is remotely the case, I couldn't help but be sickened by the thought that Rachel's life could potentially be more difficult based on the politically violent history of where she lives.

Since I visited Belfast, I've been to other countries with a politically violent history that also happen to lack decent wheelchair accessibility outside of city centers. I thought of Rachel, and I wondered what life was like for wheelchair users in South Africa during apartheid, and even now. Would a white man help a Black wheelchair user and vice versa? What about a Palestinian and an Israeli? A Syrian loyalist and Syrian rebel?

I want to think positively and believe that the first instinct wouldn't be for someone to ask questions about religious or political affiliation before offering to help someone in need. However, while a total stranger in Belfast might assist Rachel (or me) with something simple like opening a door, or even helping her get back in her chair if she falls, I know it might be a different story if it came to marriage or playdates.

I love so many things about Belfast, and I can't wait to go back, especially with my kids. However, I'd be lying if I said

Belfast didn't leave me with many uncomfortable feelings. This wasn't my country, and it wasn't my culture. But we all know what hate looks like, and it's even more unsettling when it appears in a highly unfamiliar form. By having that experience with Rachel, I now had a personal connection to someone living in a now-unspoken conflict. This took the history lesson during my city tour from abstract concept to concrete reality. Yet, I'm grateful for it because it was one more opportunity to learn about another wheelchair user's lived experience. It was also a reminder that knowing someone's personal beliefs or positions should never be a prerequisite to my expressions of kindness or compassion.

13 WHAT THE HELL? IN THE HOLY LAND

I'm not exaggerating when I say that a visit to Israel is filled with no small amount of intrigue, and a subtle (but undeniable) undercurrent of imminent danger.

In early November 2017, my best friend Erin and I embarked on a 12-night Mediterranean cruise out of Rome that would take us to various spots in Greece and two ports of call in Israel. We were excited about Greece, but Israel was the real crown jewel in our itinerary. Erin and I were both raised as Catholics, so we were extremely eager to see the presumed locations for so many of the Bible stories we'd heard during the course of our lives. We also have an appreciation for Judaism and Islam, and thought it would be fascinating to see the epicenter of convergence for the world's three largest religions. Little did we know how much of an adventure that would soon become.

The itinerary had us stopping in the Israeli ports of Ashdod for an overnight and a full day in Haifa. I worked with a local accessible tour company for a few months to set up our three days there. Our guide, Eli, suggested we book a hotel room in Jerusalem (roughly an hour east of Ashdod) for the night to save us some driving time between the city and the port for our tour the following day. Then, we arranged for a full-day tour of the Old City inside Jerusalem, which would begin shortly after our ship docked.

Our cruise ship docked on time, so Erin and I

disembarked to meet Eli on the dock at 8 AM sharp. We looked around, but we couldn't find his accessible van anywhere. We waited and waited, and still no tour guide. After some confusion and miscommunication, Eli finally showed up at 9 AM. Erin and I were a little frustrated, but we were just happy to get the day started. Unfortunately, after about fifteen minutes of driving, Eli realized he had forgotten some important documents that we would not be able to enjoy our day without. After arranging to meet up with someone to retrieve his documents, we finally got our tour started two hours late at 10 AM. These details may sound mundane right now, but…just sit tight.

After about forty-five minutes of driving, we arrived at the entrance to the walled Old City in Jerusalem. It's a very good thing we were traveling with a tour guide because the Old City is like a maze. Not only do you have to know it well to get to where you're going, but you have to know it well to remember where all the ramps are located for wheelchair users. That maze is also divided into four sections: the Jewish quarter, the Christian quarter, the Muslim quarter, and the Armenian quarter. Each one looks, feels, smells, and sounds completely different from the others.

It's hard to explain how surreal it is to be rolling around the historical part of a city that is literally thousands of years old. Yet, you're looking at modern restaurants and stores packing the passageways that cater to locals and tourists alike. The Old City is home to several significant religious sites, such as the Temple Mount and Western Wall for Jews, the Church of the Holy Sepulchre for Christians, and the Dome of the Rock and the al-Aqsa Mosque for Muslims. Even though we were there well off-season, the quarters were packed with a combination of religious pilgrims, locals, and curious tourists.

It's also difficult to overstate how intense an experience it is to be in the Old City. People and tour groups constantly move past each other in tight quarters through narrow stone alleys, either waiting in line to visit a religious landmark or clamoring for empty seats at a sidewalk café. There are notable contrasts in ambiance between the sites and the quarters. The Christian quarter was wide open and quiet, but inside the Holy Sepulchre, the sounds of people talking, praying, and crying were often deafening. At the Western Wall, visitors are divided by gender, with a black barrier separating the two. The female side was eerily quiet, with only the sounds of whispered prayers on either side of me as pilgrims approached to insert their prayer notes in the cracks between stones. All of it was everything I had imagined and expected, and so much more.

The Armenian and Muslim quarters were more intense still, with music blaring out of every shop and the smells of pungent spices wafting out of every corner. Everyone was animated, loud, and seemed to have something important to do. Tourists crammed into passageways barely wide enough for two people, and we felt lucky that I could squeeze through in my electric scooter on many occasions.

We finished our visit to the Old City around 5:30 PM, and since our tour was scheduled to end at 6 PM, I assumed we would just be heading back to the ship. However, because we started our tour two hours late, Eli offered to take us to Bethlehem—which wasn't part of the original tour—as a way to make up for the lost time. Erin and I looked at each other and quickly agreed to the impromptu detour. We were even more excited because we would be visiting a Catholic icon store, and Erin and I knew we would be able to buy a bunch of stuff to take home to our family members.

I want to take this moment to tell you, dear reader, that I am reasonably proud of my knowledge of geography. I have my weaknesses, particularly in Africa and Southeast Asia, but I can probably name at least 50 percent of the world's countries on a map. I can also look at a map of the Middle East and identify all of the countries in the region simply from having worked in counterterrorism while I was in the Air Force. That being said, I'm embarrassed to say that I was wholly unfamiliar with the geography *within* Israel—something that would have worked to my advantage on this particular evening.

Shortly after heading out from Jerusalem toward Bethlehem, the sun went down and night fell quickly. We couldn't see too much outside the van windows other than the city lights. However, the van soon began to slow and we got into a line of cars. Peeking out the windows to see where we were, Erin and I quickly made out a massive concrete wall at least thirty feet high with a guard tower illuminated in an eerie shade of green. I looked at her with eyes wide as saucers and just asked her, "Where in the hell are we?" She replied, "I see some soldiers up ahead. I think we're at a border checkpoint." *But, the border of what???*

Dear reader, in case you didn't already know this (like Erin and I didn't at the time), Bethlehem is located inside the Israeli-occupied Palestinian territory of the West Bank. This small piece of land on the west bank of the Jordan River has been under Israeli occupation since 1967. It's split into 167 "islands" under partial Palestinian National Authority civil rule and 230 Israeli settlements into which Israeli law is "pipelined." In case you haven't heard, one of the most significant conflicts in the entire world is the question of the two-state solution for Israel and Palestine. Basically, the Palestinians want their own country, want Israel out of territory they consider theirs, and the Israelis don't want to leave. The most important thing you need to know for the purposes of this story is that, for this reason, violence breaks out every so often in the West Bank between Israeli settlers and local Palestinians.

That obviously makes things difficult for people who live there, but can also make things challenging for travelers and tourists. Some of the most significant religious sites for Christians, Jews, and Muslims are located inside the Palestinian territories where violence is known to break out. My parents were already freaked out enough when I told them Erin and I would be spending three days in Israel. I told them it would be no big deal; we would be staying away from places like the West Bank. And yet, there we were.

As soon as we passed through the checkpoint, the scene around us changed dramatically. To our right was a wall extending as far as the eye could see, ostensibly separating us from a settlement. It was covered in the most beautiful graffiti I'd ever seen, reminiscent of the artwork spray-painted on the Berlin wall. To be sure, it was political art, and so much of it could easily merit a space in a museum somewhere. What made it more fascinating—and heartbreaking—was the effort the artists must've put into their work, knowing it could be washed away or painted over at any moment. To our left was a cacophony of light and sound, small storefronts with neon signs in every window and blaring loud music through their open doorways. I had no idea where we were going, and Erin and I were too timid to ask Eli where he was taking us. We just shrugged and assumed he knew what he was doing.

After a roughly 20-minute drive, we arrived at an extraordinary store owned and managed by a friend of Eli's. The owner, whose name I can't recall, is an Arab Christian, and he sells every variety of Christian icon you could possibly think of. But before we could examine his wares, I had to get inside the store. He had considerately placed a diamond-plate metal ramp outside the doorway to allow wheelchair users to enter—except for the fact that the ramp was angled at roughly 45 degrees. We soon discovered this posed no problem whatsoever, as the owner just grabbed two random young men who happened to be walking by for assistance. After a little bit of muscle and a lot of laughter, Erin and I made it into the store.

I'll never forget what the owner said to us. "You are free to look at everything, and you are not obligated to buy anything," he said. With a smile, he added, "However, you are required to share some tea with me." With cups of delicious hot tea in hand, Erin and I spent the next hour just taking in all of the amazing things on the walls and shelves: mother of pearl nativity scenes, olive wood carvings and rosaries, beautifully painted religious icons, and gold and silver crosses in every imaginable shape and size, just to name a few. I love traveling solo for so many reasons, but I frequently have moments when I wish my parents could be with me because I know they would love something in particular that I was experiencing. This was definitely one of those moments. We loaded up our baskets with goodies for our families and shared some lovely parting conversation with our highly gracious host before getting muscled out the door and down the ramp, more or less the same way we came in.

However, we now had a small problem. Eli couldn't park his van along the curb near the store, so he had to go get it and very rapidly load us in right next to an extremely busy roadway.

If you've ever observed the process of getting a wheelchair user loaded into a bus or van, there is nothing rapid about it. Just like the store owner, he recruited two young passersby to run interference for us and make sure we didn't get hit by a car (or several cars) while crossing the street to get into the van. There was noise everywhere from loud car radios and traffic and people just talking and yelling, I was internally freaking out, and all I could think was, *I'm holding a large bag filled with religious icons and I need them to get me in the fucking van in one piece.* If their job was remotely related to protecting their bearer, it was time to ACTIVATE.

After what seemed like the longest five minutes of my life, we finally got safely secured in the van and on our way back to Jerusalem. That is, until after only ten minutes of driving, we hit a very long traffic jam. We had officially entered the line to get back through the checkpoint. Although Erin and I were pretty hungry and eager to check into our hotel, we just pulled out our phones and started doing the social media thing to pass the time. We started joking around about how my parents would lose their minds when I told them (much later) we had been in the West Bank, and would ultimately be disappointed because the visit had overall been uneventful.

That was when we saw the first car in the caravan.

Certain things make a lot of sense when you see them in your home country (for me, that would be the United States). For example, if I started seeing a seemingly endless caravan of cars pass by filled with young men hanging out of windows while screaming, I would assume that somebody's team won the football game. That assumption would be bolstered by all the flags attached to those cars, and maybe even huge banners with the image of a football player attached to the sides of some of those vehicles.

Except we weren't in Kansas anymore. The flags attached to several of these *dozens* of cars displayed two fists holding what appeared to be two crisscrossing AK-47s. And those banners? At the time, I wasn't sure who that young Arab man was in the huge photos, but I was pretty sure he wasn't wearing football jersey.

Erin and I *really* started getting nervous. Our timidity flew out the window, and we immediately asked Eli what the *hell* was going on. He seemed entirely unconcerned by the situation and just casually suggested it might be a wedding party. I took one look at Erin and just muttered under my breath, "You have *got* to be kidding me." I worked in the counterterrorism field for eight years in the Air Force and four years after that as a civilian contract analyst. While I don't consider myself an expert on Middle Eastern affairs, I know enough to recognize the beginnings of a potentially volatile situation.

My heart started beating faster as the cars kept coming and flying past us on the two-lane road from the direction we were traveling. I was waiting for the sound of automatic gunfire to start any minute. If it did, there wasn't much we could do. We were stuck in a traffic jam, sandwiched between cars in front and behind. Even if Eli had the time to unload me so we could leave the road and seek shelter, he couldn't deploy the wheelchair ramp due to lack of space behind the van. All of my protective service training from my time as an Air Force Special Agent came rushing back to me, and I quickly realized that we were what they call "on the X." Even more quickly, I knew that we had no way to get off of it.

As the seconds ticked by, we continue to inch forward in line toward the checkpoint, and the caravan kept coming. Fortunately, we didn't hear any gunfire, and upon closer inspection, all the men hanging out of the cars appeared to be happy yelling, as opposed to angry yelling. After what seemed like an eternity, the last car in the caravan sped by, and things outside the van quieted down. Erin and I started speculating right away about what that entire situation meant. But before we could get on our phones to start doing some image searching, we reached the checkpoint. We asked Eli what we should do, and he just suggested that we have our passports ready. However, he said that his passengers had never been inspected in twenty years of being a tour guide.

You know exactly where this is going.

We came to a stop, and two border police officers approached the driver's side window. They were young and looked friendly, and engaged in what seemed to be a pleasant conversation in

Hebrew with Eli. He showed them a bunch of documents, which they took their time perusing. The male officer then came around to the van's passenger side and slid open the rear sliding door. Erin and I waved hello, and he very nicely asked to see our passports. He kept looking between our passports, us, and my electric scooter, which occupied a significant portion of the van. I was sitting in the rear seat next to Erin and not in the scooter (i.e., looking like a "normal" person), and he just had this look of confusion like he couldn't figure out why one of us would need a scooter in the first place. I was also trying to put myself in his shoes, and my counterterrorism experience reminded me that my scooter battery pack might be a good place to hide things that go boom.

Erin and I felt it was best to stay quiet and speak only if spoken to. After several minutes of his eyes darting back and forth, I guess the guard reached some sort of internal conclusion that my scooter didn't pose a national security threat to the State of Israel. He and his female colleague chatted a little bit more with Eli, and after that roughly 10-minute delay at the security checkpoint, we were on our way to our Jerusalem hotel.

Erin and I were starving by the time our tour with Eli ended, and I think we didn't really relax until we were seated for a lovely alfresco dinner at a restaurant around the corner from our hotel. We laughed a lot about our adventure over great food and several glasses of wine, then finally remembered to take out our phones and do some searches to learn what that caravan was all about. It didn't take long for us to figure it out, and both of our jaws dropped when we did.

The yellow flag displayed on so many of the cars in the caravan was our first hint. The hands gripping two rifles, the Palestinian flags, and the grenade in between led us to Fatah. Founded in the late 1950s by Yasser Arafat, Fatah (a.k.a. the Palestinian Liberation Movement) was the first exile group to launch attacks against Israel. It lost its majority in the Palestinian parliament to Hamas in 2006, but still controls the Palestinian Authority's presidency. Armed struggle and terrorism have historically been a part of Fatah's ideology. Still, while it maintains several armed factions, it's no longer regarded as a terrorist organization and now solely exists as a major political party. I can't tell you how grateful we were for this particular slice of information.

Mind you, Erin and I didn't exactly know these details at the time. We did a little more digging into the day's news, and we discovered that the man pictured on all those banners attached to the vehicles was a Fatah member who had just been released from an Israeli prison. Not exactly a football victory, but their team definitely felt like they won that day.

Looking back, we realized we weren't in any serious danger that day. However, we were still in a country that was on constant alert for rocket launches and terrorist attacks. Erin and I were both on active duty in the Air Force during the 9/11 attacks, but this was different. We didn't know 9/11 was coming, and while it was a massive attack on three different locations on the same day, after some time, we felt reasonably safe going back to life as usual. It wasn't like that in Israel. In Jerusalem, it wasn't unusual to see armed IDF (military) soldiers in parts of the city. While everything appeared calm like any other major tourist destination, I knew in the back of my mind that something bad could happen at literally any moment. For example, just five months before our visit, two Palestinian terrorists opened fire on Israeli police officers in the Old City. Two months after our visit, Israeli soldiers shot and killed three Palestinians in three separate January incidents in the West Bank.

I'm used to feeling physically vulnerable as a woman in a wheelchair, especially because I'm typically traveling by myself. But it's extremely rare that I feel helpless in a foreign country as an American, or because I find myself in the wrong place at the wrong time. Sure, this brief sojourn into Bethlehem makes for an interesting travel story, but how often do we find ourselves in the middle of another country's geopolitical conflict? When we read about problems that other countries are having, they seem so abstract, whether those issues are international or domestic. And because we usually don't take the time to really dig into the history of those issues, we only know what we hear and see on the news—resulting in things like my parents freaking out over this trip.

The Israel-Palestine conflict is only one of hundreds, if not thousands, around the world that are specific to one geographic area. Some people avoid traveling to places with these conflicts out of fear, and some actually seek them out. Erin and I made an educated pro-con decision to visit Israel, and specifically Jerusalem. But looking back, I don't know that I would have felt comfortable going into the West Bank had I known about the geographical details of Eli's plan ahead of time. Was there really that much danger to us as American visitors? Was it any worse than the criminal or mass shooting threat in an American city? How many of my preconceived notions were shaped by American media, or did I have a reason to be concerned based on my counterterrorism experience?

One thing I know for certain is that Erin and I would have been deprived of the magical experience in that religious shop and the owner's tea had we declined the detour. So many people in so many neighborhoods around us were living with fear and violence and conflict regularly. Yet, here we were, having this peaceful and joyous moment in a Palestinian store with an Arab Christian who shared a great friendship with an Israeli Jew. Being able to recognize that as it was happening might have been the most surreal moment of a complete Alice in Wonderland day.

I'm happy to say that our second day spent visiting Masada, the Dead Sea, and Judea, and our third day visiting Galilee, Capernaum, and Tiberias, were completely uneventful from a conflict perspective. It was incredibly strange to see all of these places from the Bible where Jesus lived and walked and did his thing, and I'm not even a practicing Catholic anymore. Just from a historical perspective, their significance was overwhelming. I was very grateful for the peace of these places, although the intensity remained; it was just of a different nature. Erin and I were even more thankful for the full day at sea we had following our departure from Haifa, as we needed to massively decompress from our Israel experience.

Since our trip to the Holy Land, I've been to other countries with regions plagued by conflict, both geopolitical and terrorism-related. When I read or hear news about events or attacks in those regions, it holds so much more meaning for me—

largely because I now understand both sides of the conflict, even though I was exposed for only a short time. I've also had the privilege of meeting people at both ends of it. As a foreign visitor, I didn't feel it was my place to choose a side, then or now, and I could see how complicated and personal the issue was for everyone involved. Any conflict where people on both sides are getting killed is rarely as simple as outside observers imagine.

So, long story not-so-short, I do not have the solution for peace in the Middle East. However, I have learned that it's best to wait to tell my parents about any related future endeavors until after I get home.

14 HAVE FORGIVENESS FOR HAVANA

In April 2019, I secretly visited Havana, Cuba, and lied to my parents about it until after I got home.

I know this sounds weird and makes me come across like a horrible daughter, but I promise you, I had very good reasons for this. It all goes back to the 1960s, the crazy story of how my parents got out of communist Cuba, and how they feel about their homeland now. I can't explain the cloak-and-dagger nature of this trip until I tell you a little bit about their history.

My entire family is from Cuba, and while my relatives came from a few different parts of the island, both of my parents' lives were centered in Havana. When the Cuban Revolution started in 1959, everything went to hell in a handbasket for a lot of people very quickly. My father's family lived on a military base called *La Cabaña*, and while my mother lived in Havana proper, her family had a farm outside of the city. I remember her stories of how her sisters would have to grab her by each arm, being very pregnant with my older brother, and rush through their fields to escape the distant sounds of bombs and gunfire. Soldiers were descending from the mountains into the city, and nobody knew what was going to happen. People who refused to pledge loyalty to the revolution were being thrown in jail or publicly executed.

As Fidel Castro settled in as Cuba's new communist dictator, tensions rose between the United States and the island country. After all, we were in the middle of the Cold War with the

Soviet Union. After being rejected by the US government, Castro found a willing ally in the Soviets, who very much valued a base of operations in the Caribbean so close to its American enemy.

History books tell us that the closest we've ever come to a nuclear holocaust and World War III is the Cuban missile crisis in 1962. While the entire world was on edge trying to figure out what was going to happen between Kennedy and Castro and Khrushchev, my family was also in the midst of crisis. Then-President Kennedy had initiated a naval blockade of Cuba while my dad was at sea as a naval engineer with the Cuban merchant marine. My parents and infant brother didn't know it at the time, but when my dad left for that voyage, it was the last time they would see each other for two and a half years.

Not knowing when they would have another opportunity, my father and several other officers aboard his ship requested political asylum while docked in Canada. Because the situation in Cuba was relatively new, the Canadian government wasn't set up to grant them asylum. However, he was able to negotiate legal residency in the United States through the Embassy. He was sponsored by some relatives we had in New Jersey, although it was still eight months before my mother knew where my dad was or even if he was still alive.

In the meantime, the Cuban government viewed my father as a deserter, and as punishment, refused to let my mom and infant brother leave Cuba to reunite with him in the US until 1964. Even then, my mom had to leave through Mexico, and the process of getting their exit papers was a weekly ordeal for her for almost a year. The only reason the government finally granted her permission was that, while holding my crying infant brother during her forty-sixth trip to the immigration office, she broke down into *very* loud sobs in front of a Chinese delegation that was visiting that day. To avoid embarrassment, the immigration official finally shoved her exit papers across the desk.

There is so much more to their story, and most of the time, I feel completely incapable of putting the anguish of their journey into exile on paper. Suffice it to say, it was an extremely traumatic experience. As such, my parents have vowed never to return to Cuba until the communist dictatorship that forced them to leave is toppled. It's been roughly fifty-seven years since they left, and they haven't seen the shores of their homeland since. This is the backdrop against which I was raised in South Florida in the late 1970s.

I've always been very close to my parents and have the utmost respect for them and their experiences. During the 1960s and early 1970s, almost my entire family ended up emigrating from Cuba to South Florida, so I was constantly surrounded by rapid-fire Spanish (technically my first language), Cuban food, and salsa music. I was lucky to live so close to my grandparents, aunts and uncles, and many cousins, all of whom were born in Cuba (until me). Because of where I grew up, particularly so close to Miami, my family has always been very anti-Castro, anti-communist, and everything that goes along with that—specifically, being pro-embargo.

Decades ago, the US Congress passed laws that prohibit virtually all financial support of the Cuban government. For most of the past sixty years, it has been illegal to purchase things like Cuban cigars or Cuban rum. If you're lucky enough to get a visa to visit Cuba, you're not allowed to stay in any hotel or eat at any restaurant owned or controlled by the Cuban government. American companies have mostly been prohibited from doing business in Cuba. While the extent of these prohibitions has fluctuated over time, particularly in the last decade due to political changes here in the United States, the embargo is still in effect and can only be lifted by an act of Congress.

This is totally separate from what I like to call the family embargo. Out of respect for my parents, their views, and their experiences, my brother and I had similarly vowed not to visit Cuba until it was no longer a communist country. We took this promise very seriously, and I always gave stern warnings to any friends contemplating a visit after travel restrictions started to loosen up under President Obama. I always made sure other people understood that their money was propping up a communist dictatorship, and their tourist dollars would do very little to help the Cuban people. I also urged them to try to open their eyes to the sad reality of life in Cuba and look beyond the beautiful beaches, cabaret shows, and vintage cars.

When I became a wheelchair user, I assumed that Cuba would permanently be off-limits to me. Accessibility can be challenging in some parts of the United States, and a virtual impossibility in a developing country where finding a functioning wheelchair is as tricky a task as renting a unicorn for your kid's birthday party. A few years ago, my fears were confirmed when I read a magazine article about a group of wheelchair users who sailed to Cuba in an accessible catamaran. Two of them were manual chair users, so they were a little more flexible getting around Havana. However, they had to rent an ambulance to get their power wheelchair-using friend around. I can't even begin to describe the harrowing experiences he had trying to use makeshift ramps to get him up any number of steps.

While my MS progressed, I felt pretty certain that I would never have the opportunity to visit my family's homeland, as the Cuban government didn't seem to be going anywhere in a hurry. When travel to the island began to open up, I started to get really jealous of all the non-disabled travel writers, friends, and family members who were visiting Cuba and having a great time. My FOMO (fear of missing out) grew exponentially when the number of cruise ships stopping in Havana also began to grow. Still, I was reminded of the promise I made to my parents, as well as my disability and the lack of accessibility in Havana.

When January 2019 rolled around, I felt that my tiny sliver of opportunity to visit Cuba was about to shut down for good. The Trump administration was cracking down hard on the Cuban government by rolling back many of the normalization policies former President Obama had put into place. I knew it was only a matter of time before the US government would ban American cruise ships from visiting Cuban ports, and given the fickle nature of US politics, there was no way to know if or when they would ever start back up again. Flying to Cuba and staying in local accommodations was completely out of the question for my accessibility needs, so a one-day stop in Havana on a cruise would be my only option to plant my wheels on Cuban soil.

I had a big decision to make. My version of multiple sclerosis is progressive, so I already knew I had a limited amount of time during which I could safely travel anywhere. I was also betting that the communist government in Cuba would probably last longer than my mobility. On the other hand, I felt I would be betraying my parents by visiting Cuba and going back on the unspoken promise I made as a young girl. I had never felt so torn in two directions by a decision in my entire life. How could I pass up the opportunity to fully explore my heritage and see the place that defined the stories passed across family kitchen tables throughout my childhood? Would it be worth potentially hurting my parents and irreparably damaging our close relationship?

But before I could even contemplate making such a decision, I had to figure out if I could even manage to see a tiny bit of Havana in my wheelchair. I scoured the Internet for blog posts or videos by other wheelchair users who had attempted such a trip. Unfortunately, they were few and far between. I knew accessible transportation would not be an option, but because my power wheelchair comes apart and fits in a trunk, I would be able to use a regular sedan taxi. Luckily, I found a local tour company that was willing to work with me and my mobility limitations. They explained we would split the four-hour tour in half, with two hours spent rolling around Old Havana, which is pedestrian-only, and the other two hours doing a driving tour around the city.

Now that this Cuba trip was becoming a real possibility, I had to decide whether or not to pull the trigger. I needed advice.

The first person I called was my brother and my sister-in-law, whom I knew were still dead set against visiting Cuba. If I decided to go, they would eventually find out, and I didn't want them mad at me as well. Needless to say, I was nervous about speaking to them, but I felt like the conversation could help me predict how my parents might react. Fortunately, they understood my internal conflict, but they also knew that this might be my only chance to go. They were supportive, and it also helped to talk to my uncle, who had visited Cuba multiple times with my aunt to visit her family members. I finally talked to two of my closest friends, who helped me work through both sides of the debate. After all, I knew that no one was going to decide for me. I had to come to a conclusion for myself. After weeks of agonizing, I decided to go.

Because I knew Havana would be a real physical challenge, I enlisted my close friend Lori to come along with me on the *Norwegian Sun*. This itinerary would take us from Port Canaveral, Florida, to Key West, then to Havana, then back to Port Canaveral over four days. We would pull into the Port of Havana before sunrise and stay docked for a full twenty-four hours before heading home. I hesitated for only a split second before clicking on the button that said BOOK NOW.

Yeah, that word.

NOW.

Now, I just had to figure out what to tell my parents.

The first quarter of 2019 was a busy travel time for me, and I had three other cruises booked for that time frame. My parents have a hard time keeping track of all my trips, so I figured it would be easy for this one to get lost in the mix. As late April approached, I vaguely told them I was going on a short cruise with Lori to Key West and Cozumel that I snatched up at the last minute because of a great sale. I had also never sailed with NCL before, and as an accessible travel writer who specializes in cruises, I was on a mission to sail on all the major cruise lines. They quickly forgot about it, and the day before I went to pick up Lori on our way to Port Canaveral, they wished me a safe trip and told me to send them lots of pictures.

Pictures. *Hadn't thought about that part.*

I was already anxious when I picked Lori up at her house on our day of departure. We had been talking extensively about the trip and how significant it would be for me, so she could feel my nervous energy. It helped that Lori had visited Cuba twice before on land tours for extended visits, so she walked me through what I could expect to see and experience. It also helped that she practices Buddhism, and she patiently shares with me so many customs and rituals that help me relax and be grateful for every experience and opportunity—including the ones that bring me anxiety.

The first two days of the cruise were glorious, with sunny weather and a lovely visit to Key West. I grew up visiting the Florida Keys with my family on fishing trips and spent a considerable amount of time in Key West as a college student in

Miami. However, it was my first time visiting as a wheelchair user. We had so much fun seeing the butterfly conservatory, watching the six-toed cats at the Ernest Hemingway house, and eating freshly-made Key Lime pie at 10 AM.

Even though Lori and I knew we'd have an early morning the next day for a 6:30 AM arrival into Havana, we stayed up late talking. I was restless, and I knew I wouldn't get much sleep. I was already awake when my alarm went off at 6 AM. I wasn't really in a hurry because we wouldn't be getting off the ship until several hours later. However, I wanted to see whatever I possibly could in the darkness as we sailed into port. Lori had already woken up and left our cabin in search of some coffee, and we agreed to meet up on the top deck. It was about half an hour before sunrise, and all I could see were the lights on the hills on either side of the shipping channel. It took a while to approach the dock, and as the sun came up, I could see more of the surrounding landscape through the fog. It started to hit me that I was actually looking at Cuba.

I'm not exactly sure how to explain this feeling or sensation. The best way you can relate is to think about something you've heard about for your entire life. It can be a person, or a distant land, or a toy, or a movie. Anything. You've seen pictures of it, you've heard stories about it, and you know people who have either been there, or lived there, or seen it, or used it. You've built this idea in your head of what the experience would be like to see this concept firsthand, but it's always been through the lens of somebody else. Then, the moment finally presents itself, and BOOM!...you're not sure what you feel. It's very anti-climactic, I promise you. You're waiting for this big *MY GOD!* moment, or tears, or some other major emotional outburst, and it doesn't come. What did come, for me, was simply a peaceful smile, and calm anticipation for what would happen next.

Shortly after breakfast, the time came for Lori and me to disembark our ship and make our way through Cuban immigration. Lori had been through this process twice before at the airport, but I was paranoid for an entirely different reason. Even though it's been decades since my parents left Cuba, they rely on stories from the island to form their opinions on how things go when people visit in the present day. Also, because of how my dad left Cuba, he's worried that Cuban authorities might try to arrest me or detain me or take away my American passport if they found out I was his daughter. Even I think that's a bit of overkill. But Cuban intelligence was indeed trained by the KGB back in the day, so who knows what they're looking at?

I was thinking about this as I nervously approached the immigration officer seated behind Plexiglas in a small compartment. *Would he take forever going through all the pages? Would he have questions about the dozens of passport stamps from all of the world? Would he look at my last name and know from a quick scan that my ex-husband is in the US military? That I had been in the military?*

Yeah…not so much. The immigration officer didn't even look at my passport's photo page. He literally found an empty space, stamped it, and passed it back accompanied by an extremely dour expression telling me he would rather be anywhere else but inside that little compartment. This was the first sign that my brief visit to Havana wouldn't live up to the Cold War intrigue that my dad had built up in my head. "Security" consisted of half a dozen very young women wearing uniforms comprised of short khaki skirts, fishnet stockings, and patent leather high heels. They took one look at me, probably decided they weren't sure what to do with me or my wheelchair, lightly ran their hands over my arms, and told me I could proceed. Lori and I just looked at each other like, *What in the hell was that?*, and just continued to move through the terminal.

After exchanging our US dollars for the local currency, we crossed the street and met up with our tour guide, Marco Antonio. The friendly 27 year-old local had a big smile on his face, greeted us warmly, and we liked him immediately. Over the next two hours, he took us on a walking and rolling tour of Old Havana, which was much easier to navigate than I anticipated. To appease the growing masses of tourists arriving in Havana on cruise ships, the Cuban government spent a lot of money turning that part of the city into a pedestrian-only area, replacing rough cobblestones with pavers and sprucing up the façades of crumbling buildings. Most tourists who visit Havana only see the beautiful exteriors and the window dressing, but I knew the secrets behind those walls, as Lori and I would come to confirm later. In the meantime, my head was on a swivel, trying to absorb every inch of scenery in front of me. I don't think I've ever taken so many pictures and so much video in one place in my life. After all, this wasn't just for me. This would spawn hours of conversation with my parents after my return.

After our tour's walking portion, we hopped into a modern taxi Marco had reserved for us for the driving part. We cruised along *El Malecón*, which is a famous broad promenade bordering the sea. Some of the most iconic photos of Havana feature the waves crashing against and over this seawall. We drove through *La Cabaña*, the military base where my dad and his siblings were born and raised. We also drove by Cuba's capitol building, which ironically is modeled after the US Capitol in Washington, DC. There were so many other streets and neighborhoods we saw during that windshield tour that brought back memories of so many conversations with my parents over the years. It was like drinking from a fire hose, and all I could think over and over again was, *So, this is what [insert landmark here] looks like…*

Our incredible tour with Marco ended around 3 PM, but our day wasn't finished. Because wheelchair accessibility in Havana is practically nonexistent and good food is scarce, we went back to the ship for a late lunch and so I could safely use the bathroom. US law at the time stated that all cruise ship passengers had to be part of a tour group to visit Havana. Having just fulfilled that requirement, we were able to head back out into the old city around ninety minutes later for some independent exploration.

During this free time, Lori and I felt a little bit more comfortable interacting with the locals. Even though Marco told us plainly that things have changed a lot in the last few years and he felt free to do and say things publicly that we thought were unlawful, we were still anxious about getting him in trouble. For a long time, Cuba has been the kind of place where they will put you in jail for criticizing the government. Only having my family as the primary source of information about happenings on the island (for better or worse), I couldn't help but be paranoid. At first, we were nervous about taking photos of the military soldiers posted on virtually every block because we believed this was forbidden. But upon closer inspection, we realized these soldiers were just kids—barely out of high school, in very ill-fitting uniforms, and bored out of their minds.

I met an older man who was a double amputee, sitting in an ancient metal wheelchair that was barely held together with bungee cords and duct tape. Despite both the chair and its occupant clearly having seen better days, the man was smiling, laughing, and absolutely fascinated with my power wheelchair. We spoke at length in Spanish, shook hands, and took plenty of photos together. He had a straw hat where he was collecting donations from passersby. It mostly contained coins, but since I had plenty of money, I gave him ten CUCs, roughly the equivalent of ten US dollars. That doesn't sound like a lot, but that money could feed a small Cuban family for a week or more. I didn't give him more because I was worried that the police would take the money away from him if they saw it in his hat.

As Lori and I continued in our quest for more photos, videos, and human interaction, we were occasionally approached by locals asking if we had any toiletries or fresh food to give them. Not money; nobody asked for cash because they knew they could get arrested if they got caught doing so. They wanted shampoo and toothpaste instead. Milk. Soap. Things that Americans buy for pennies and take for granted every day, but are worth their weight in gold in a communist country.

We finally got away from the touristy part of Old Havana and crossed the street to where the locals live. The roads were in terrible shape with potholes everywhere, and every third building looked like it had been subjected to a targeted earthquake. The Art Deco and neoclassical façades were dirty and decrepit, telling tales of sad nostalgia while overlooking the rubble behind padlocked fences. We saw *bodegas* where locals could only buy food with a ration card; a few solitary cans and bags of rice on the shelves under the watchful eye of a guard. We saw a group of teenagers playing handball against the wall of a crumbling apartment building, and half a dozen rowdy men gathered around a small square table playing *Dominó*, the cracking thunder of marble violently meeting wood that was the soundtrack of my childhood.

Lori and I had agreed we would head back to the ship when it got dark, and it was hard for both of us to believe that our Cuban experience was so quickly coming to an end. We had a long dinner spent just talking about the day, with Lori mostly helping me decompress and process everything I had seen and felt. I explained that part of me felt guilty for not feeling the emotional weight I thought I was supposed to carry going into this day. My entire experience was positive and exciting, although I felt I had done my familial duty by making an effort to see Havana's real underside that my parents always spoke about.

She just smiled, and explained that it wasn't my job to see Cuba through the lens of my parents or my family members, or anyone else. Despite the horrible ordeal my parents went through to leave Cuba, I had to remember that their years living there up until that point were pretty awesome. Of course, I could take their stories with me, but that journey had to be my own. Hearing Lori explain it that way lifted a massive weight off my heart. However, I still had a huge emotional hurdle to clear—I had to tell my parents where I had really been.

After returning from any trip, my parents always come over to look at all my pictures and see what fun little souvenirs I brought for them. This case was no different, except that instead of excitement for our visit, I felt a truckload of anxiety. I truly had no idea how they would react. Would they be upset, angry, happy, disappointed, sad…? A combination of these things? The handful of family members I told about this trip ahead of time for safety reasons tried to reassure me, but I had no way of knowing how my parents would react until I spilled the black beans.

"You know how I said that Lori and I were going to Cozumel after visiting Key West?" I began tentatively. "Well…we didn't actually go to Cozumel." After I said that, I gauged their initial reaction, which was surprisingly one of concern, thinking there was something wrong with the ship or we had somehow gotten deviated from our intended course.

Okay. Suck it up, buttercup.

"We went…to Havana."

And there it is, folks.

My parents were both initially silent, and then their facial expressions quickly turned to ones of surprise. My dad let out an astonished, "WOW!" My mom covered her mouth with her hands and said, "Oh, my God!" But then they started...smiling. And laughing. "You *really* went to Cuba?" my mom asked incredulously. I told them right away that we went there on purpose, and I had been planning it for a few months. I quickly apologized for not telling them, but I was worried they would be upset (or worse, disappointed) with me for going or concerned for my safety. I also reassured them that my brother, sister-in-law, aunt, and uncle all knew I was going and where I would be at all times.

Our conversation proceeded very quickly after that. They asked me a million questions about where we went, what we did, what we saw, and what the experience was like for me. They were happy and excited for me, and the anxiety I had been feeling for months quickly melted away. I queued up on my TV the video I had made and the photos I had taken, and we must've spent at least two hours going through all of them.

Then something magical happened. Every few photos or every thirty seconds or so in the video, my mom or dad would tell me something about their connection to that specific place. For example, my mom would say, "Oh, that's only a few blocks away from where I would walk to school every day," or, "The apartment we lived in was down that street over there." During the portion of the video that showed *La Cabaña*, my dad recognized the houses where people he knew used to live, and the names of most of the buildings we passed in our taxi. Hearing these things made me feel so much more connected to both my heritage and my parents. Places that felt distant and abstract for forty years of my life suddenly became real and concrete with just a five-minute video.

I intentionally didn't buy many souvenirs because most of the money goes to the communist government, and very little of it goes to the actual salespeople. However, there was no way I was coming back from this once-in-a-lifetime trip empty-handed. I gave them a few little things, and I was amazed and that we had all been so light-hearted up until that point. That all changed when I gave my mom a very special gift.

The patron saint of Cuba is *la Virgen de la Caridad del Cobre*, or Our Lady of Charity. My grandmother had a life-threatening experience while in labor with my mom, so everyone prayed to Cuba's patron saint for a safe delivery. Although everyone calls her Cary, this is why my mom is named Caridad. During our tour with Marco, we passed in front of the Cathedral of the Virgin Mary of the Immaculate Conception. I've amassed quite a collection for my mom of religious icons from around the world since she is a devout Catholic. There was no way I was leaving Havana without bringing her something relevant to her namesake.

I was able to buy for her, with Lori's physical help, the traditional image of *la Virgen* inlaid on a piece of wood. This is a significant custom because, according to legend, three men in a rowboat found the original statue of the patron saint attached to a board after a huge storm had cleared. It was a beautiful design, and as soon as my mother unwrapped it, she started crying. Which meant that I started crying, and I generally don't do tears. I was so grateful for the chance to *know* my parents in a way I hadn't before. It was just a beautiful moment with them that I'll never forget.

Six weeks after Lori and I returned from our cruise, the US government prohibited all cruise ships departing US ports from visiting any Cuban ports. Several cruise lines had to start a massive scramble to rearrange their itineraries—many of them in progress because the Trump administration at the time didn't provide much advance notice of the cruise ship ban. Fast-forward two years to the present day: cruise ships haven't started sailing yet because of the COVID-19 pandemic, but the ban remains in place.

It's unclear if the current Biden administration will reverse the ban on cruises to Cuba, or any other travel restrictions to the island that have been imposed over the last eighteen months. By the time you read these pages, cruises may have restarted in some parts of the world. However, based on the glacial pace of geopolitical change and the distinctly more rapid pace of my MS progression, it's unlikely I'll be able to visit Cuba again. Despite the stress and anxiety that came along with me on this trip, I wouldn't do anything differently, as it represents some of my greatest travel memories.

Trust me; I second-guessed my decision to go on this cruise *a lot*. But it has reaffirmed my conviction that, if you have the financial, logistical, and physical ability to travel to a bucket list destination, you have to do it without hesitation. *So* many things can change in an instant to close off that destination to you for a long time: a military coup, policy changes, natural disasters, a personal or family illness or injury…the list goes on and on. Having made a choice to visit Havana, now I can't imagine the emptiness I would feel never knowing my family history, or having my parents pass away (in hopefully many years' time) without making that special connection.

My pipe dream is that by the time my sons are old enough to travel independently in a decade or so, they'll be able to visit a free and democratic Cuba easily. However, I'm a practical person who understands history, so at this point, I just hope they can visit legally. I can also only hope to inspire in them the same sense of wonder, curiosity, and passion about their heritage. Whether it's the island on that poster in your office, your family's homeland, your seventh continent, or the theme park of your kids' dreams, don't put it off—especially if you don't have to confess to your parents when you get back.

ACKNOWLEDGEMENTS

This book started its journey many years ago. While it didn't reach its intended destination, I'm eternally grateful to my literary agent Diane Stockwell at Globo Libros for her eternal support and encouragement.

What started as a loose collection of stories came together into a cohesive gathering of memories and lessons, thanks to Kelsey Tressler. I don't envy her mission of sucking every possible emotion out of my body and infusing it into this book, but I think it worked.

Many of the adventures in these pages wouldn't be possible without the assistance of incredible accessible tour companies and guides around the world, many of whom have been significantly impacted by the pandemic's impact on travel. I'm grateful to have kept in touch with most of my guides, many of whom have become friends. Special thanks to Mirjam, Veroniek, Gerda, Miha, Danijel, Roger, Paul, Jenny, Olivia, Antonio, John, Margaret, Anna, Sergio, Eli, Rene, Ivy, Marco, and Javeed.

I was able to safely get from point A to point B literally hundreds of times around the world because of my trusty Whill Model Ci and Pride UltraX. I'm grateful to both of these companies for their dedication to advancing mobility technology for people with disabilities.

I'm lucky to be part of an amazing community of wheelchair users and disability rights advocates. Thank you for reading my words about accessible travel in all their different forms and locations, and for supporting and encouraging me every (figurative) step of the way.

Much love, abrazos, and besos to my parents and family for your unending support, and for always praying for me every time I leave the house. Erin, Alana, Azure, and Lori, you already know you fall under the family category, and I love you all.

I reserve the most significant and heartfelt gratitude for my two sons. Traveling with a wheelchair mom is different and a little more work, but you make every trip unforgettable. I love you more.

ABOUT THE AUTHOR

Sylvia Longmire is an award-winning accessible travel writer and photographer, author, bilingual voice actor, producer, entrepreneur, and disability rights advocate. She is also a service-disabled US Air Force veteran, full-time wheelchair user, single mother, and the former Ms. Wheelchair USA 2016.

Ms. Longmire is the founder of the Spin the Globe accessible travel blog, on which she shares her adventures traveling solo around the world in a power wheelchair. She focuses on the wheelchair accessibility of her destinations, encouraging fellow wheelchair users to explore the world. Her accessible travel writing has been featured in *The New York Times, New Mobility* magazine, and Lonely Planet, and she has published four accessible travel-related books.

Ms. Longmire is also a subject matter expert on Mexico's drug war and border security. She is a frequent guest on major media outlets, providing interviews for CNN, MSBNC, FOX News, NBC Nightly News, and more. Ms. Longmire has been a guest expert on The History Channel's *Brad Meltzer's Decoded* and *America's War on Drugs*, and has also consulted for producers of the National Geographic Channel's *Border Wars* and *Drugs, Inc.* series. She is the author of two books on these issues.

Her on-camera work (and COVID-19) led to a career pivot and the exciting start of a new career in voice acting. Her newest business, Wheels Up Media, combines her explosive start in voiceover with on-camera, print, and online media work. She is currently producing and directing a TV documentary, animated short film, and hosted accessible travel series under development.

Ms. Longmire is the President and founder of The PreJax Foundation, a 501(c)(3) non-profit that provides scholarships to exceptional students who either have MS or a parent with MS. She is a single mother to two amazing boys and resides in Central Florida.

FOLLOW SYLVIA LONGMIRE

SPIN THE GLOBE
www.spintheglobe.net

FACEBOOK
Facebook.com/spintheglobeonwheels

INSTAGRAM
Instagram.com/sylvia_longmire

TWITTER
Twitter.com/spin_theglobe

YOUTUBE
Youtube.com/smlongmire

OTHER BOOKS BY SYLVIA LONGMIRE

Blogging While Disabled: How to Make Money Writing From a Wheelchair

Everything You Need to Know About Wheelchair Accessible Cruising

The View from Down Here II

The View from Down Here

Border Insecurity: Why Big Money, Fences, and Drones Aren't Making Us Safer

Cartel: The Coming Invasion of Mexico's Drug Wars

Printed in Great Britain
by Amazon

85262585R00075